CW01033100

LONDON'S RIVER

Eric de Maré

LONDON'S RIVER

The Story of a City

With drawings by
Heather Copley and
Christopher Chamberlain

THE BODLEY HEAD
LONDON SYDNEY
TORONTO

ISBN 0 370 00846 4
Printed and bound in Great Britain for
The Bodley Head Ltd
9 Bow Street, London WC2E 7AL
by Unwin Brothers Ltd, Woking
Set in Monophoto Baskerville
First published 1964
Reprinted 1965
Revised Edition 1972
Reprinted 1975

CONTENTS

CHAPTER I

Before the Buildings

THE Romans invaded Britain and built a bridge across the Thames nearly two thousand years ago. Ever since then the place where the bridge was built has been important. It grew into the largest port in the world—so large now, that the wharves of the many docks, where sea-going ships tie up to load and unload their cargoes, add up to a total length of more than seventy miles.

Many who live in London do not realise that their great city exists because it has always been, and still is, above all else, a riverside port. It is not as easy to see this now as it was in the past, because London has spread so far away from the river which gave it birth that to travel today by car or train from its centre into the open country can take over an hour.

Most Londoners are now cut off from their river by grimy brick walls and warehouses, and they make little use of it. But for much of the time that London has existed the river played a big part in the daily lives of its citizens, for they were never far from it and they used it as a wide high-street.

At the time Christ was born, and before the Romans conquered Britain, all the land on which London now sprawls was wild country. The River Thames was wider than it is today, and so it flowed along more slowly. Its banks were clean and gravelly, and its water was clear and full of fish; even great silvery salmon swam there.

On the higher ground above the banks, thorn bushes and brambles grew among trees, but all the lower land was marshy and covered with reeds, through which many streams wandered towards the river. There the wildfowl nested and the wading birds strutted.

The river came winding from the west through a green valley.

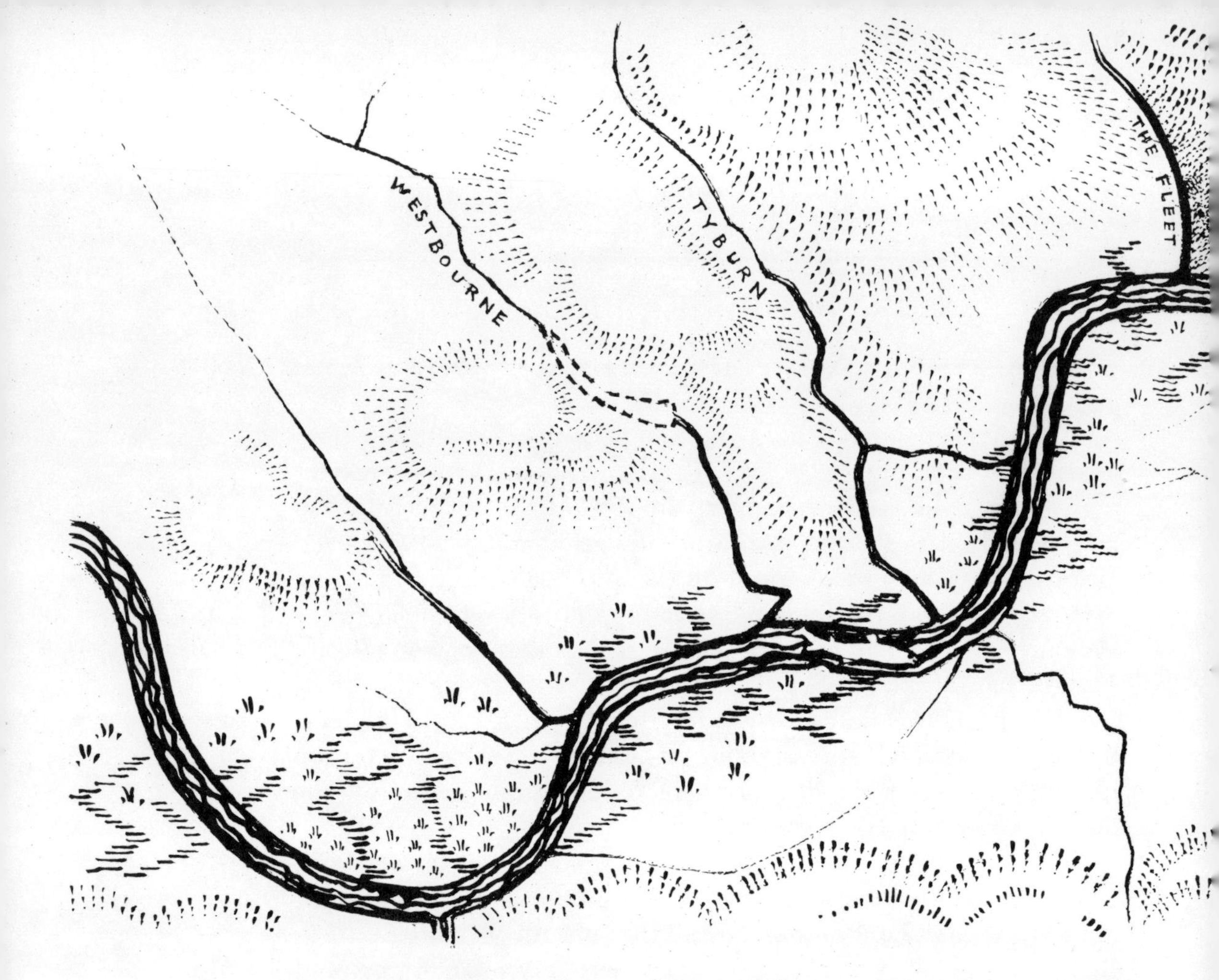

It began in what is now called Gloucestershire as a bubbling spring, 160 miles away. For some way it flowed along as a small brook, which often dried up in the summer months. Then, as one stream after another added to its waters, it grew in size, until it passed through a gap in a range of hills at a place now called Goring in Oxfordshire. Thence it flowed into the wide valley known today as the London Basin, where it continued to grow in size as it collected the rains running down from the hills to north and south. At last the banks curved away from each other round the flat marshes of the estuary, and the river became one with the open sea.

At a place some forty miles before the river joined the sea, two low, rounded hills covered with trees and bushes rose on the north

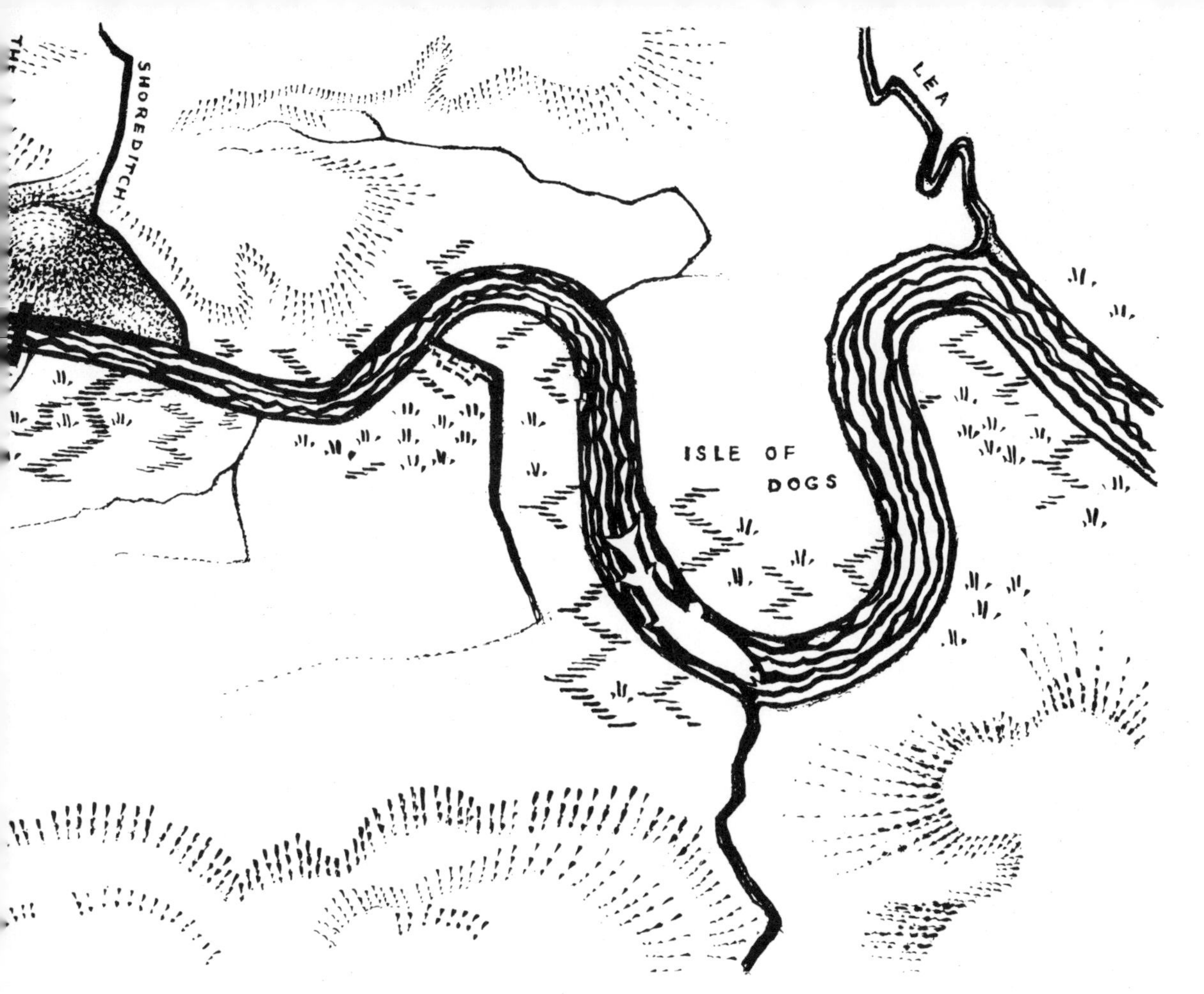

The Thames River at London with its tributaries. At the centre of the map on the north bank are the two hills, divided by the Walbrook stream, on which the ancient City stands.

bank, and there London was to be. On the top of the eastern hill Leadenhall Market stands today, and on the top of the western one St Paul's Cathedral.

About five miles to the north-west some high ground covered with forest arose, where Hampstead and Highgate now lie, and from these hills three streams came winding down to join the river. The one nearest the western hill has been called by several names through the centuries—River of Wells, Turnmill Brook (when it turned some water mills), and the Holbourne, while the part nearest to the Thames became known as the Fleet, meaning a place where ships can float.

About two miles farther to the west, another stream, which was to be called the Tyburn, ran through the marshes. Before it reached the Thames, it divided in two at a spot very close to where Buckingham Palace is now. It is believed that the two streams formed an island having the Thames on one side of it, and this came to be called Thorney Island. There today stand Westminster Abbey and the Houses of Parliament.

The third stream, and the one farthest from the western hill, is now called the Westbourne. Today part of it makes the Serpentine Lake in Hyde Park and Kensington Gardens, and as a drain it trickles unseen into the river near Chelsea Bridge.

In the valley between the two hills on which the future city was to rise, ran another, and very short, stream, which acquired the name Walbrook, while on the other side of the river to the south ran several other brooks.

All these tributaries were covered over in later times, and so, although dips in the ground will sometimes show where they ran, they cannot be seen today. For centuries, however, they were open to the sky and were in daily use, some for shipping and all for supplying water. Then in time they became too shallow and dirty to be used for these purposes, but many of them still serve today as underground drains and sewers.

About four miles to the east, where the Thames began to loop round an area of marsh now called the Isle of Dogs, a fairly large river flowed down from the north to join the Thames. It is called the Lea. On either side of its mouth now lie the largest enclosed docks of London's port.

Before London existed, clusters of huts made of wattle and daub with roofs thatched with reeds were dotted here and there in the landscape. Around them banks of earth were sometimes thrown up, topped by stockades of logs, for protection against wild beasts and enemies, while cattle grazed nearby, and corn grew in a few surrounding plots. On the river and streams men fished from small round boats made of bent sticks covered with skins, called coracles.

Most people in Britain lived by farming, fishing and hunting, while a few lived by their skills in making things for use or decora-

A coracle.

A village of the early Britons with its round huts and surrounding protection.

tion. They could weave cloth, make pots for cooking, and beautiful jewellery, decorated hand-mirrors, swords, knives and shields of iron or bronze. Though their lives were rough, their leaders dressed magnificently in flowing robes of woollen cloth, colourfully dyed and ornamented with brooches of bronze or gold.

No British nation then existed, and the people belonged to separate tribes. They were often at war with each other, and would charge into battle in two-wheeled chariots drawn by pairs of trained horses.

These were the people the Roman soldiers had to fight and to conquer when they landed in Britain.

A war chariot.

CHAPTER II

Roman Bridge and Port

In 55 B.C. Julius Caesar raided south-east Britain from Gaul with a small army. He returned the next year and fought his way against the fierce tribesmen across the River Thames, right into the area now called Hertfordshire. But he departed that autumn, and nearly a hundred years passed before the Romans attacked Britain again.

This time they conquered the whole country as far north as the Scottish border. It took them forty-one years of fighting with their spears, shields and short swords fully to subdue the tribes and to capture their hill forts, but after that they ruled a peaceful country for nearly four hundred years.

In A.D. 43, then, in the reign of the Emperor Claudius, the Roman soldiers landed on the south-east coast, and, marching north-west, came to the Thames. The river divided a large part of southern England from the rest of the country to the north, and somehow the Romans had to cross it. At first they may have done so by fording it where it was shallow, and the ford may have been where Westminster now lies. Soon they may have built a temporary pontoon bridge—that is, one having planks laid across a row of anchored boats. Or they may have used ferry boats.

However, as the conquest of the country went on, more and more traffic arrived from Gaul and Rome—officials, merchants, slaves, and especially marching soldiers with all their heavy weapons and equipment. They all had to cross the Thames on their way to the midlands, west and north. A bridge was badly needed, and it was soon built.

The Roman engineers knew by long experience what they should look for. It was a spot where both banks were suitable for bridge-heads, and which was as near as possible to the sea and to Europe,

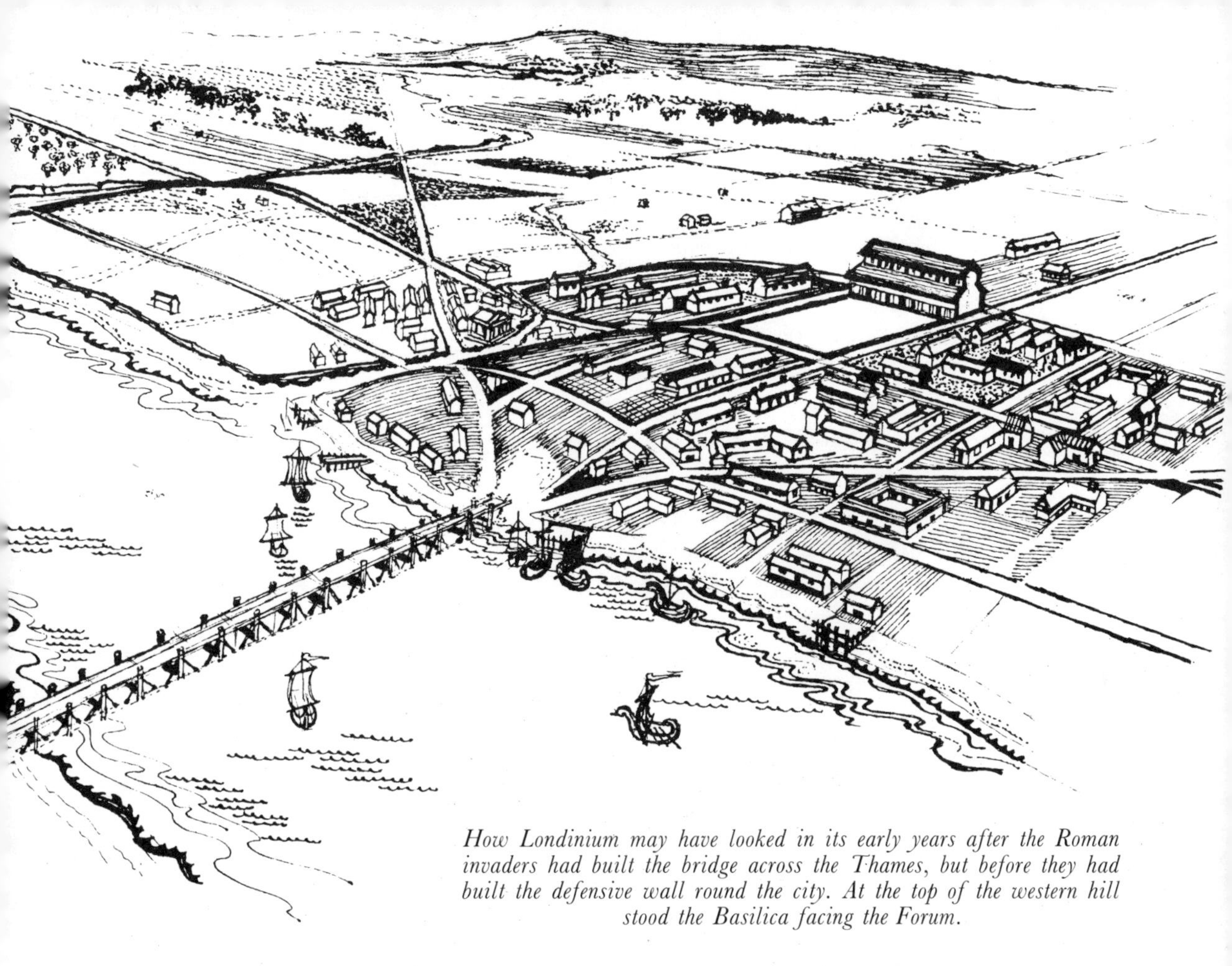

How Londinium may have looked in its early years after the Roman invaders had built the bridge across the Thames, but before they had built the defensive wall round the city. At the top of the western hill stood the Basilica facing the Forum.

so that long journeys to the west could be avoided. They found only one suitable site. It was at the foot of the twin hills, for there two dry, gravelly places, rising just above the soft marshes, faced each other across the river; nowhere else along the river banks towards the sea did two such firm patches of ground face each other. So there the Romans were able to build a bridge, and, because villages and towns always grow where a bridge has created a meeting place, there London was to develop.

The bridge stood almost at the same place as the London Bridge we know today, which runs to the foot of the eastern one of the City's two hills.

Apart from its firm banks, the spot chosen for the bridge could, on the north bank at least, be easily defended. Streams surrounded the two hills like a moat, while all around lay marshy land which an attacking army would find difficult to cross. It was also a good site in other ways. Ample water was there for drinking and washing, fish could be caught for food in the river and streams, timber for building could be cut down in the nearby woods, and ships from the Continent could be sailed up the river to the bridge, helped by the tides.

Eighteen years after the Romans had landed, a fairly large port had grown around the north end of the bridge. Wharves, warehouses, streets and houses stretched from the Walbrook in the west to a point on the east near which the Tower of London stands today. Most of these early buildings, like the bridge itself, were of wood, for that was a plentiful, quick and easy material to use.

A few buildings also stood at the south end of the bridge, and may, indeed, have been erected before those at the north end. If so, Southwark could claim to be older than London City itself.*

* The name Southwark means South Work, or south rampart, and was first recorded in A.D. 1023.

A closer view of early Londinium by the bridgehead.

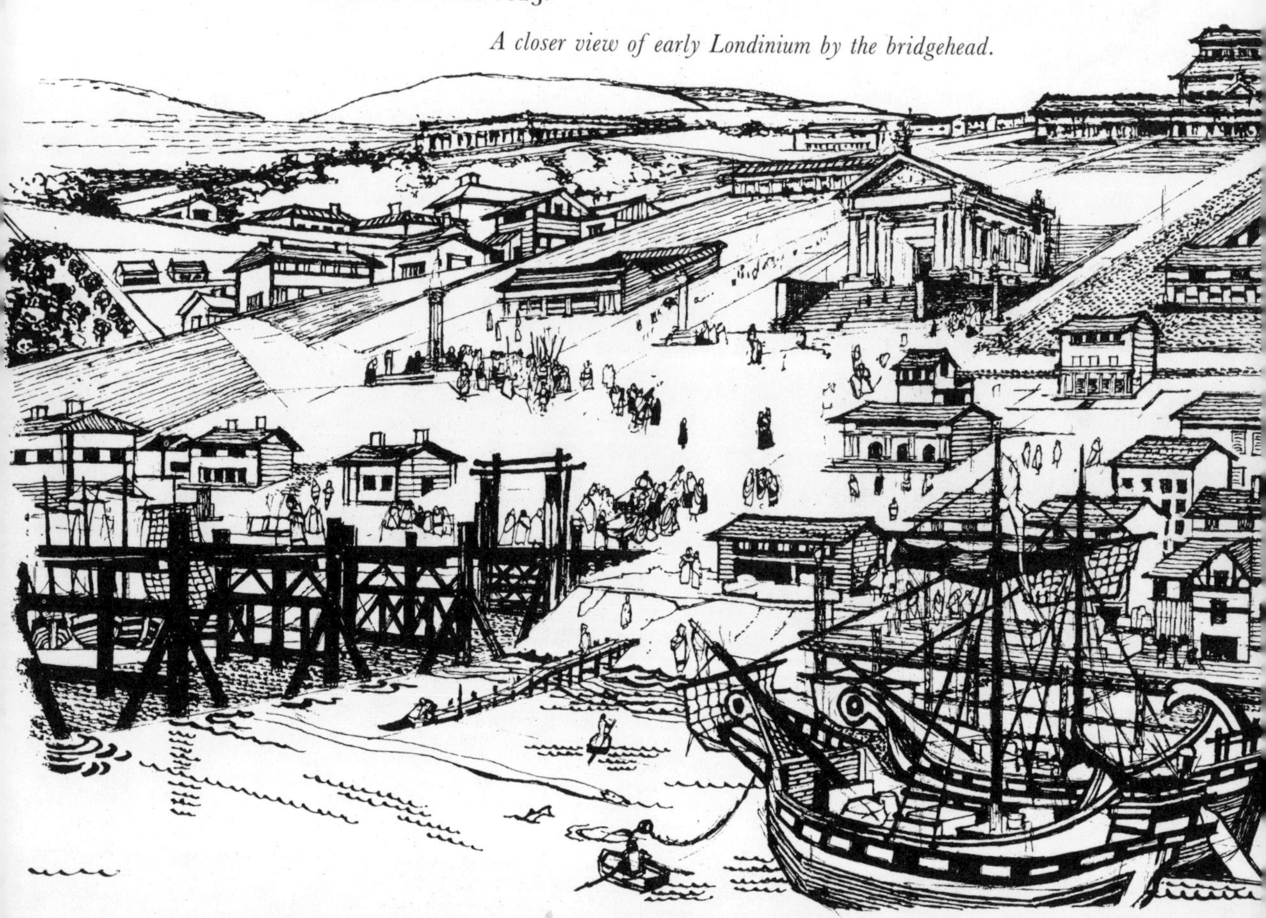

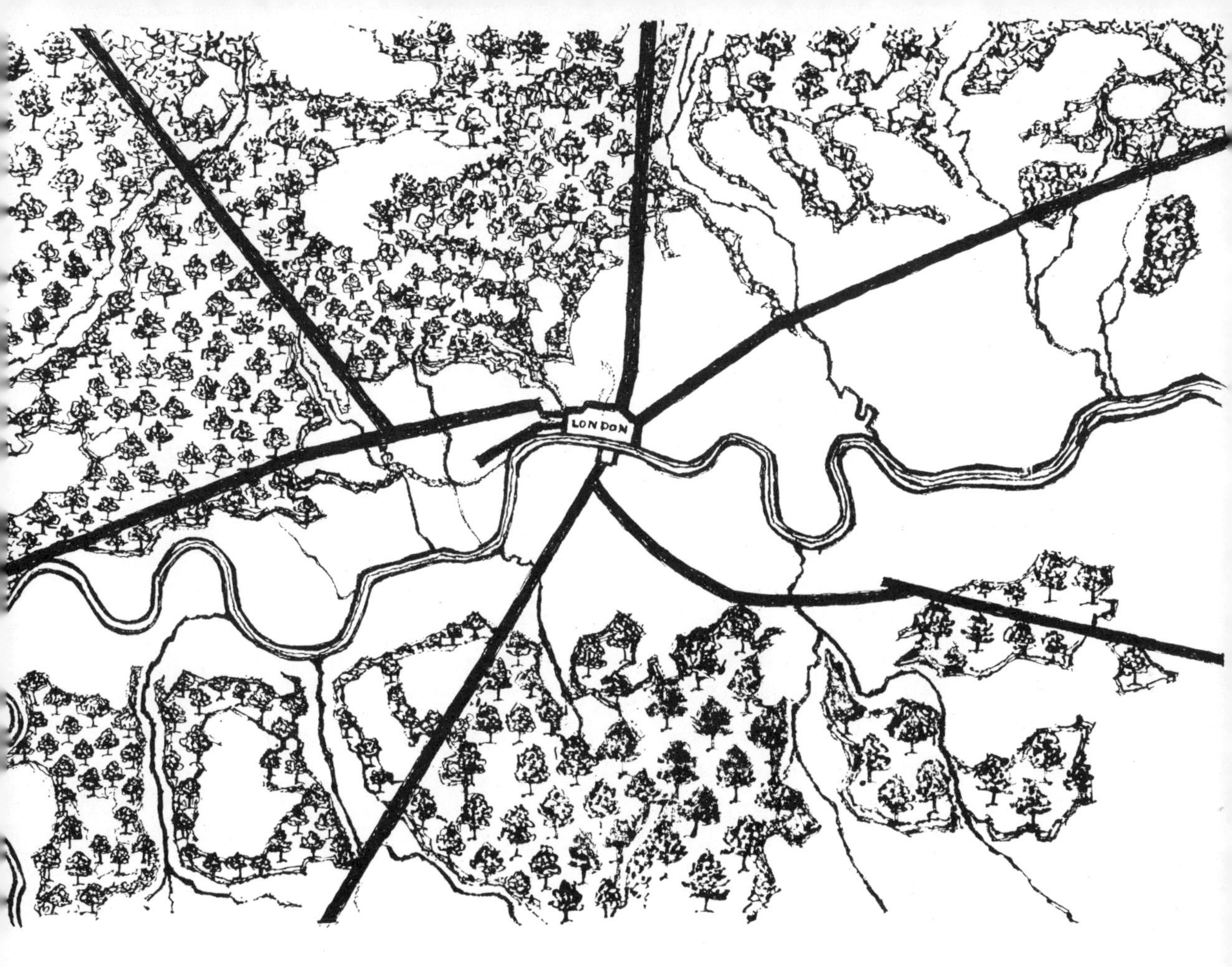

Map showing how the straight Roman roads ran towards Londinium and its bridge. The lines of many of these roads still exist; for example, that running down from the left-hand top corner of the map is now the Edgware Road.

Although it always had its own militia for defence, London was not at its Roman start, and never became, an important military centre. It is even doubtful that it was a government centre until the Middle Ages, and then the seat of government was not in the old City but at Westminster, lying two miles to the west. London was, from the beginning, a centre for trade. Before long, six major Roman roads ran in their straight way towards its bridge from different parts of the country. London became not only the largest town in Roman Britain, but one of the great trading cities of the world. So it has always remained.

In A.D. 61, only a few years after its foundation, London suffered its first calamity. The tribe of the Iceni, enraged by the cruelties of the Romans, and by the exorbitant demands of their tax gatherers, revolted against the invaders. Led by their Queen, Boudicca, and her charioteers, they swept down from Norfolk, killing, torturing and burning on their way. They destroyed the whole of the new London by fire. Ashes have been found as evidence of that fire, and a heap of coins, all minted before the year 61 and fused together by heat, was discovered at the approach to the bridge.

Somewhere outside London the Roman legions made a last, desperate stand. The Iceni were defeated and Boudicca poisoned herself. But the Romans had learned a hard lesson, and after this rebellion, which nearly lost them the country, they treated the Britons better. Soon London arose again, and on a much grander scale than before. Now it covered both the hills, and a defensive wall of rough stones bonded with bricks was built right round the town, three miles long, twenty feet high, nine feet wide at its base, and surrounded with a moat fed by the streams. It enclosed both

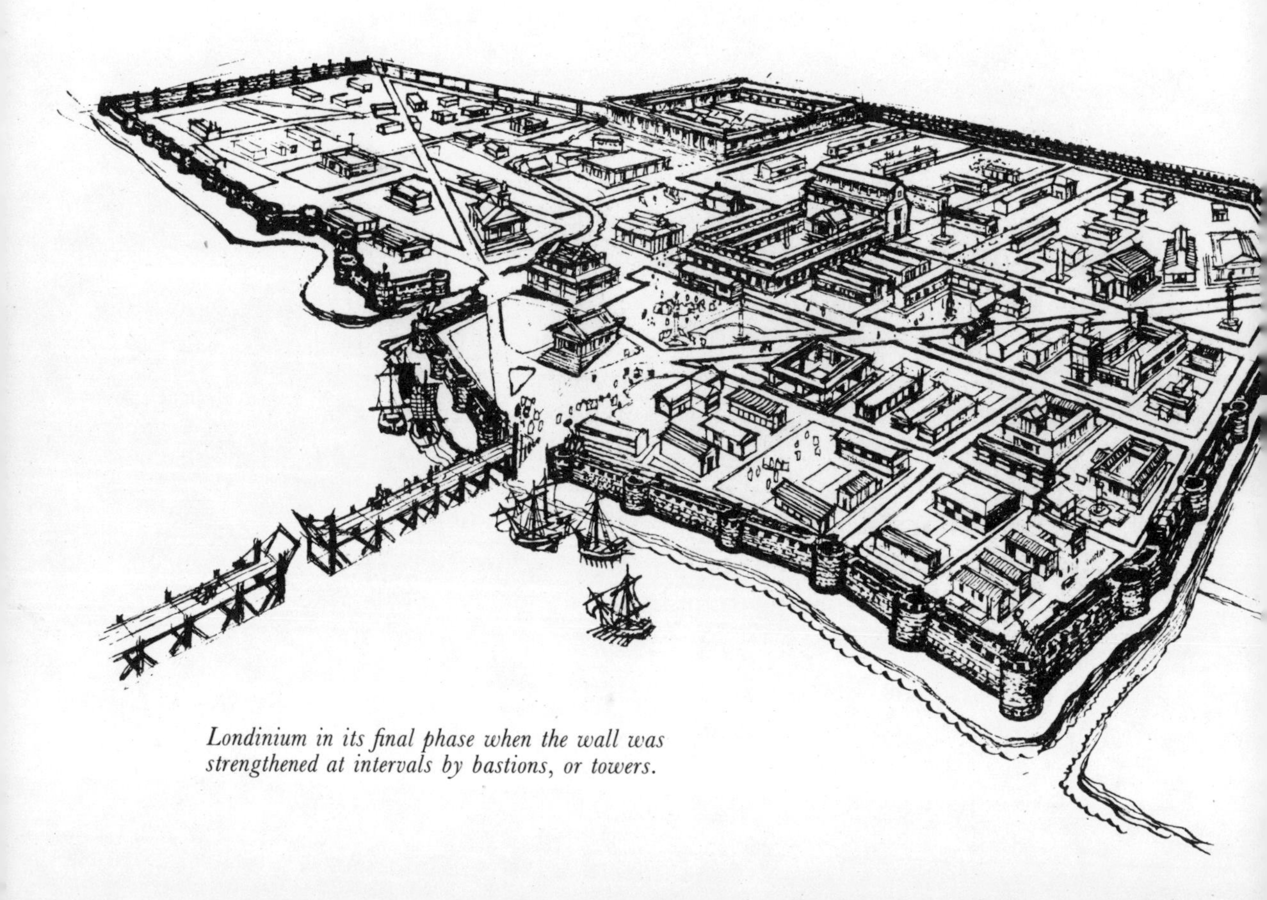

Londinium in its final phase when the wall was strengthened at intervals by bastions, or towers.

the hills, and covered about the same area as the London core we know today—the so-called Square Mile of the City.*

What did *Londinium*, as the Romans called it, look like after the wall had been built and when it had become one of the five largest Roman towns north of the Alps?†

Southwark, the settlement at the southern approach to the bridge, now covered about fifteen acres, but it was not enclosed by a wall. It had an inn or two for travellers arriving late in the day from the coast, some villas and shops, and perhaps also an arena for such sporting events as chariot races and fights between wild animals and gladiators.

The bridge was no doubt rebuilt a number of times during the Roman occupation, and always of wood. It may have had stone piers after a while, and its timbers were probably painted for preservation and decorated with bronze ornaments. The south end was defended by a tower, or pair of towers, and in the centre was a drawbridge, which could be raised by ropes or chains to allow ships, with their tall masts, to pass through.

At the north end of the bridge, where it joined the wall, stood a wide entrance to the City, with towers on either side of it. The entrance may have had two gated arches with a pier in between, for that was a common Roman practice.

Behind a line of wide, sturdy, timber wharves or landing stages, the wall ran right along the river front, and here and there it was pierced by doors and gateways to give entrance to the streets and warehouses behind. Some way to the west of the bridge along the

* Parts of the Roman wall have survived to this day and can still be seen, for instance, just north of the Tower of London.

† The Latin form *Londinium* is the first appearance of London's name on record. No evidence exists to prove that a settlement of any importance existed at London before the Romans arrived, and from which they might have taken this name. Like the name Thames, the name London may be Celtic in origin. It may come from the Old Celtic word *londos*, meaning fierce—from a Celtic family called *Londinos*—from the Welsh words *Llyn Din*, meaning the city, or fortress, by the lake—from a Gaelic compound of *Lon*, a plain, and *Dun*, a hill—or it may have been called by Belgic invaders after *Londinières*, a place in Belgium. Other origins of the name have been suggested, but no one really knows the true one.

riverside, lay a kind of bay like a harbour, where ships floated and round which the wall probably ran on three sides.* Farther west still was a wide opening in the wall, perhaps a hundred yards across, through which the Walbrook, running between the two hills, flowed into the river and provided another mooring-place for ships.

From the bridge gateway into the city a wide main road, paved with stones and rutted by chariot wheels, ran straight up the eastern hill to a large, open market-place at the top. This was the Forum. A colonnade may have run round the east, west and south sides of the Forum, and, extending all along the north side, stood the finest building in the city, perhaps the finest in the whole country. It was the Basilica, which served as a town hall, a law court and a business centre. It may have been built of stone, or even of marble, with roofs of red tiles, porticoes, a large inner court-yard, and a great central hall over four hundred feet long.

* That river bay was to be called Queenhithe. It is still there today, and is now surrounded by warehouses.

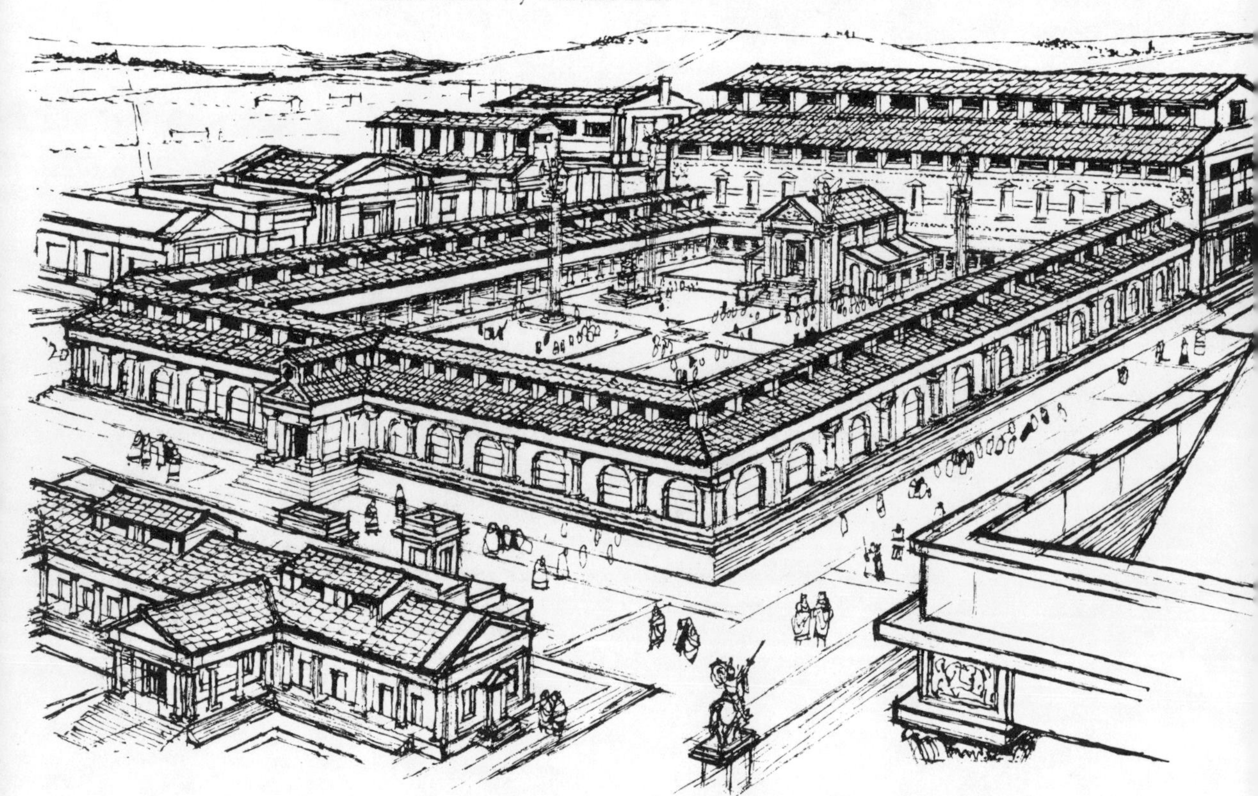

A close view of the Basilica and Forum as it may have looked when Londinium had become one of the five largest Roman towns north of the Alps. It stood on top of the more easterly of the city's two hills, where Leadenhall Market stands today.

Around the Forum, and perhaps linked by the surrounding colonnade, may have stood other important buildings—one or two temples, the Governor's house, shops and public baths, while a number of impressive statues of gods and emperors in bronze, stone or marble, set high on pedestals, stood in the Forum itself.

The streets of the town were laid out in a fairly regular way at right angles to one another, though two important roads probably ran diagonally from the bridgehead to the north-east and north-west, the latter in the direction of a large fort and barracks covering eleven acres, which had been built at an early stage on the north-west corner of the city.*

Of the buildings lining the streets or set back in plots of land, some were of squared stone, or stone through which bands of brickwork ran, but most were of brick or of rubble stone covered with cement painted in bright colours. All the roofs were of low pitch, covered with red or brown pantiles like those which can still be seen all over Italy today. Many houses were several floors high and some were decorated with carvings. Wide porticoes were everywhere and, although they had first been designed for a warmer country as protection against the heat of the sun, they gave useful shelter here against rain and wind.

The inner walls of the large villas belonging to rich citizens had bright frescoes painted on them; their inner courtyards were paved with coloured mosaics depicting subjects from mythology, and often surrounded a tinkling fountain to remind their owners of the sunny Italian homeland.† Under the ground floors of these villas were spaces called hypocausts, which could be heated with warm air from a fire in cold weather—an early form of central heating.

Several such comfortable, well furnished, and richly ornamented villas probably stood along the banks of the Walbrook, lying in green gardens and orchards sloping down to the stream. A

* The fort was in the area now called Cripplegate.

† An example of such a floor, found in Leadenhall Street and now in the British Museum, shows Bacchus riding on a panther.

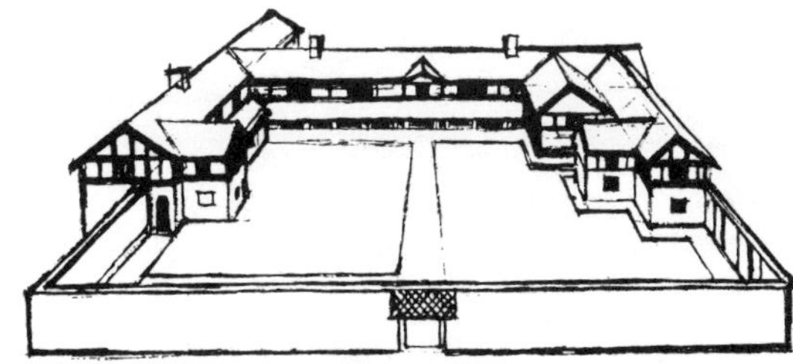

A typical Roman villa.

temple dedicated to the god Mithras certainly stood by the Walbrook, for remains of this were unearthed in 1955, when excavations for a new office block were being dug.*

The streets of this highly civilised town were lively with passing people, horses and decorated chariots. Foreign tongues could be heard everywhere, and Latin was spoken with many strange accents. Through the gateway of the bridge, a troop of legionaries might come marching in good order, on their way through the city to man the wall in the north of Britain, which had been built right across the country by the Emperor Hadrian to keep out the wild Picts. Then those walking in the streets would stand aside to watch the soldiers pass, for they were a fine sight in their glistening armour above their red tunics, and their well-wrought helmets decorated with embossed ornaments and bright plumes. Among those who watched might be a wealthy London merchant reclining in a litter carried by four slaves and dressed in the white toga of a free man.

Along the riverside wharves lay many ships, mostly manned by Greek sailors. Some were light, slim galleys moved by coloured square sails and by rows of oars. Others were heavier vessels like sailing barges. Many of the ships were finely made, with carved heads of animals and birds at the prow or stern. Those arriving from foreign lands would bring bronze-ware, such as decorated tripods on which oil lamps could stand, woven rugs and textiles, glass-ware, perfumes, olive oil and wine in huge jars with two handles, red Samian pottery, plain or ornamented, from Gaul, and all the luxuries of a complicated civilisation based on slavery and conquest. Now and then a splendid piece of sculpture, made by a skilled Roman artist to stand in the Forum, might be landed, or some bronze statuette to decorate the courtyard of a villa.

Into the holds of departing ships would go tin, lead, silver, hides,

* The mystery cult of Mithras, the ancient Persian god of light, was not unlike Christianity in some ways, and, because it stressed the virtues of courage and honesty, it was much favoured by Roman soldiers and merchants. Relics discovered on the site, a model of the remains of the temple, and many interesting finds from Roman London can be seen at the Guildhall Museum.

A piece of the Samian ware from Gaul which Roman Londoners used in their homes. Its colour is a rich browny red.

The Roman mosaic floor found in Leadenhall Street and now in the British Museum.

grain, gangs of slaves chained together, and snarling packs of hunting dogs.

By A.D. 350 *Londinium* had become so flourishing a town that it was officially honoured with the title *Augusta.* But serious troubles had been affecting the whole widespread Empire for some time. In Britain raids by pirates from the coasts of the North Sea and the Baltic were increasing, and about the year 370 the wall around London was strengthened at intervals by towers, or bastions, as added protection against the raiders, for on their flat tops could be placed the newly-invented giant catapults of the Roman army.

In A.D. 410 Rome itself was attacked by Alaric the Goth and his followers. The Emperor Honorius, trying desperately to save the tottering Empire, recalled the legions to Italy, and, by about the year 423, the last Roman soldiers remaining in Britain had marched across London Bridge on their way back to Rome. The inhabitants of London and of the other Roman towns in Britain had to fend for themselves against the raiders—so-called Scots from the west, Picts from the north, and rough, bearded Angles, Saxons and Jutes from Germany, Holland and Denmark.

A Roman soldier.

CHAPTER III

Dark Years

WHAT happened to London and its riverside during the Dark Ages which followed the departure of the Roman soldiers? Little is known. The invasions of Britain by the kindred races of Angles, Saxons, Jutes, Danes and Vikings went on for five savage centuries. The raiders—heathen worshippers of Thor and Odin—murdered, burned and pillaged without mercy, but some of them, especially the Saxons, did not want so much to plunder as to find new farm land on which to settle.

At first the Romanised citizens of London, not trained to fight and no longer part of a great empire protected by a strong, professional army, defended themselves against the raiders as well as they could. The city may have been captured more than once, in spite of the protection which the crumbling Roman wall would have given.

London became ever more ruined. Broken columns lay in the streets, bushes and trees sprouted from the cracked pavements, and grass grew over the mosaic floors of the roofless villas. Parts of the town became deserted, and in time the regular Roman streets disappeared. Skills, crafts and learning were lost, and for the squatters among the ruins life was rough, disorganised and dangerous. Houses of wattle and daub or of rubble picked up from the Roman remains were built without planning, and their roofs were thatched or shingled, because tiles and bricks were made no more. Many families left London to live in the country where life was safer, and although some of the invading Saxons eventually settled in London, most of them came to farm the land and hunt in the forests, preferring to live in the country in small family groups.

But somehow London survived, and we know from *The Ecclesiastical History* of the Venerable Bede that in the year A.D. 731

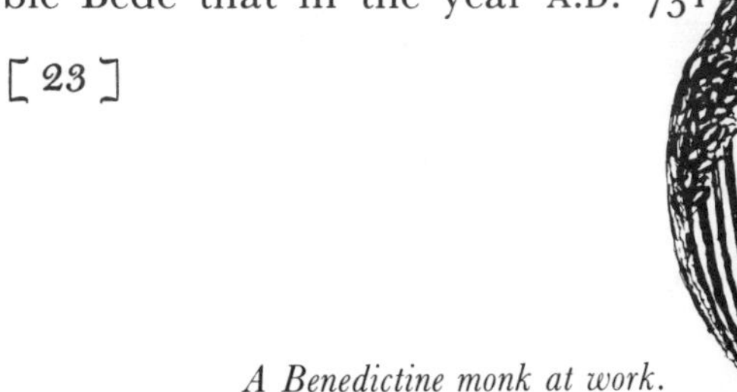

A Benedictine monk at work.

After the Roman soldiers had been recalled from England to Rome about the year A.D. 423 London fell into decay. Here is an imagined scene of the ruins. Note the rows of short columns in the pit which once

London was once again a trading port. However dilapidated they had become, the old Roman roads which radiated from London were still used, and they helped to make trade possible.

Christianity had already established itself in Roman times, and had had its supporters in Roman London; indeed, Christianity had become the official religion of the Roman Empire in A.D. 313, when the Romans still occupied Britain. With the Saxon invasions, it almost vanished but it reappeared after the missionary St Augustine landed in Kent in A.D. 597 and founded the bishopric of Canterbury. Those early Christians formed a link between the old world which had vanished and the new world which was being born, for, in the chaos, they alone preserved the language, learning

supported a floor covered with a mosaic design; warm air from a fire circulated between the columns below the floor. Called a hypocaust, this was an early form of central heating.

and crafts of ancient Rome, and were able to hand them on.*

Under the guidance of the Church with its new bishoprics and parishes, and the Benedictine monasteries with their schools, some order began to return to Britain. In A.D. 610 a cathedral named after St Paul was first built in London, and it was rebuilt sixty years later on a different site, on top of the City's western hill, where—now rebuilt for the fifth time—it still stands today. In that early cathedral many a fervent prayer was to be muttered for delivery from the fury of the Vikings.

The main Viking invasions began in the ninth century, and the

* They preserved many building methods, and in Denmark to this day bricks are called monk-stones.

worst of them occurred during the nine years between 866 and 874 when the well-armed and disciplined Danish host swept over the land, murdering and looting as they came. During this ninth century London suffered several attacks by the Danes, until Alfred, the learned Christian King of the West Saxons, drove them north, rapidly repaired the city walls and formed a city government.

Trade went on, in spite of the troubles, and many Norsemen were themselves traders, rather than pirates and marauders. All were splendid seamen, and at the London wharves their slim, undecked ships floated, with carved dragon prows proudly curving upwards, rows of oars projecting below round defensive shields, alternately black and yellow, and single square sails in coloured stripes.

We do not know if the bridge remained during the Dark Ages. For a time the one left by the Romans may have stood and have

Viking ships at their moorings.

been patched up until it became too rotten to use. After that, unless a primitive new bridge was built, the river may have been crossed by ferry, or, when it ran low in hot summers, by wading across in certain places.

However, we do know that London had a bridge in 984, because a strange report was recorded that year in Anglo-Saxon. It tells how a widow and her son had driven pins into the image of a man, of how they were discovered in this act of witchcraft, and of how the widow was taken and drowned at London Bridge, while her son escaped and was outlawed.

After that the bridge is mentioned more often in records. In the year 1014, when the Danes held London and Southwark, the Saxons under King Ethelred the Unready were joined by a band of Vikings from Norway led by their King Olaf. Together the armies sailed up the Thames to attack the bridge and divide the Danes. But the Danes stood on the bridge and hurled their spears down on the open ships, forcing the enemy to retreat. Then Olaf and his men quickly protected their ships with thatched roofs pulled down from nearby cottages, and rowed up to the bridge once more. Let the *Olaf Sagas* tell of the battle which followed:

'Between the castle and Suthwirki (Southwark) there was a bridge, so broad that two waggons could pass each other upon it. On the bridge were raised barricades, both towers and wooden parapets in the direction of the river, which were nearly breast high; and under the bridge were piles driven into the bottom of the river. Now when the attack was made the troops stood on the bridge everywhere, and defended themselves . . . King Olaf, and the Norsemen's fleet with him, rowed quite up under the bridge, laid their cables around the piles which supported it, and then rowed off with all the ships as hard as they could down the stream.'

The bridge collapsed, and the Danes lost their hold on London. It is an old tale which has stayed with us in the nursery rhyme, 'London Bridge is broken down'. Ottar Svarte, the Norse poet, gloried in it:

A Viking warrior.

'London Bridge is broken down,
Gold is won and bright renown.
Shields resounding,
War horns sounding,
Hildur shouting in the din.
Arrows singing,
Mailcoats ringing—
Odin makes our Olaf win.'

In 1016 Canute, later King of Denmark and Norway, became King of England. Danes and Saxons were reconciled, and the country, which had been divided for so long into small, warring kingdoms, was united within a loosely-joined Nordic Empire. The pirates of the North Sea were put down and the days of plundering were over. London soon became a richer trading centre than it had been since the time of the Romans.

The tomb of Edward the Confessor in Westminster Abbey.

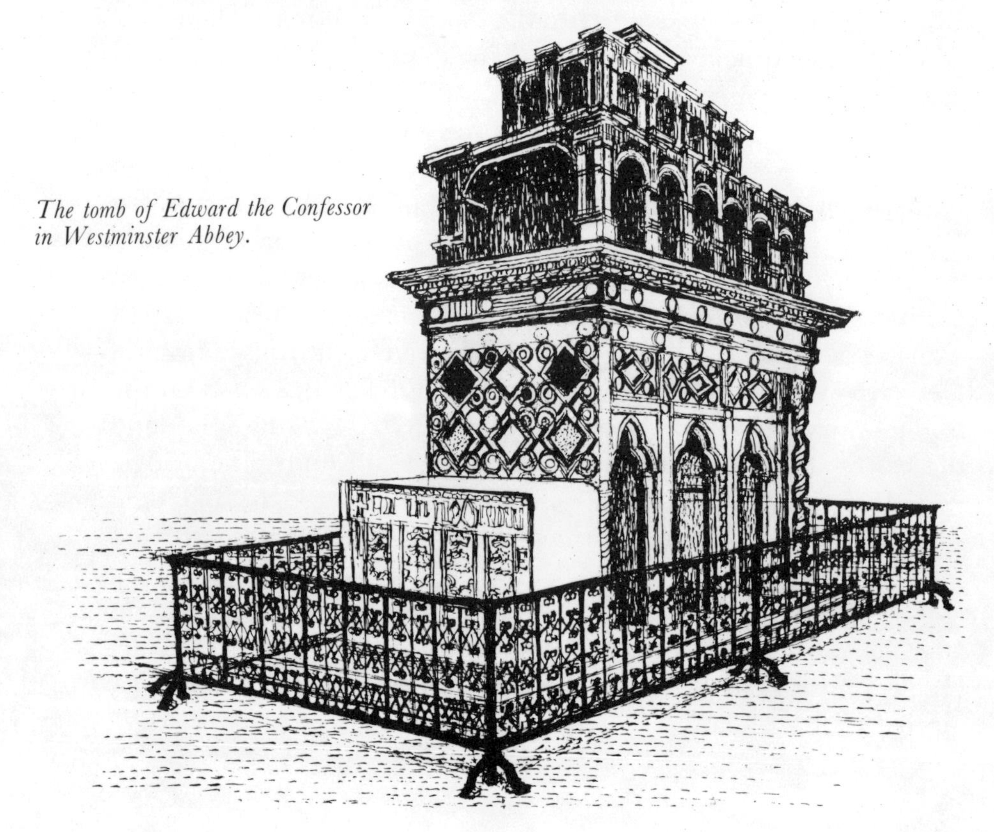

Canute died at the age of forty before he could consolidate his empire, and between 1042 and 1066 the pious Edward the Confessor, half Saxon and half Norman, reigned in England. More a monk than a king, he rebuilt Westminster Abbey, which is known to have existed at least as early as A.D. 740, and which the Danes had destroyed. He did so in the new Romanesque, or Norman, style with round-headed arches, square vaults and sturdy round columns. He also restored the royal palace, which stood close to the Abbey. He is regarded as the true founder of Westminster Abbey, and there he has a tomb. With him began that close link between Westminster and the monarchy and government of the country, which has lasted to this day. Of all the monarchs of England only two—Edward V and Edward VIII—were not crowned at Westminster.*

* Edward V, the elder of the Princes in the Tower, was never crowned, and Edward VIII, who abdicated in 1936, and became the Duke of Windsor, reigned too short a time for his coronation ceremony to be held. If it had been held, it would certainly have been in Westminster Abbey.

The oak Coronation Chair at Westminster Abbey on which all but two of England's monarchs, since the time of Edward I, have been crowned. Below the seat is the legend-bearing Stone of Destiny—the Scone Stone from Scotland

CHAPTER IV

Mediaeval City of Spires

IN 1066 Edward the Confessor died, and Harold, last of the Saxon kings, and his army of weary footmen were defeated at the Battle of Hastings by the Norman invaders from France—tough, ruthless, energetic cavalrymen, who were mostly of Viking blood. Their leader was William the Conqueror, Duke of Normandy and kinsman of the Confessor.

A new age began in England, which was to last until 1534, when Henry VIII abolished the authority of the Pope in England. During that time the Roman Catholic Church was as powerful as the King, and it owned much land and wealth. This deeply affected building and people's daily lives—not least in London.

Advancing into England with his army, the Conqueror reached Southwark, and, to show who was now to be king, he set fire to the houses there. Then, looking across the river at the walled city and at its defended bridge, he prudently marched west to Wallingford, the first place up the Thames where he knew that the river could always be forded at any time of the year. So there he crossed, and marched back to London along the north side of the river, in order directly to threaten the city. The citizens accepted the new ruler without resistance and, on December 26th, 1066, William was crowned King of England in Westminster Abbey.

Before long, and with only a few thousand armoured knights, he had subdued all of England with its population of some two million people, and he was able to reward his followers with grants of land taken from the Saxon landowners. To protect themselves against Saxon revolt, the Norman nobility built strong castles, first of wood and later of stone, and within four years of the Battle of Hastings, William himself had built his first castle. It stood on the riverside at Windsor, a day's march from London along the old Roman road which ran through Staines. From there London could be controlled until another castle could be built on the south-east corner of the City itself. Some twelve years passed before the Tower of London was completed. It was called the White Tower, because it was built of a white stone imported from France.*

The Tower of London was one of the four main riverside buildings of mediaeval London and Westminster. The other three were Baynard's Castle, a gloomy row of stone towers by the river's edge on the south-west corner of the City, named after its first Norman custodian, Rolf Baignard—Westminster Abbey lying two miles west of the City—and the King's Palace at Westminster.†

The first known description of London in the Middle Ages has been found in the writings of a monk called William Fitzstephen, who was born in London during the reign of King Stephen (1135 to 1154), but wrote in the time of Henry II (1154 to 1189). Like Thomas à Becket, whose murder he witnessed and whose biography he wrote, he was proud of his city, regarding it as a fine place, religious, well-defended, and inhabited by honourable people, handsome in both dress and manner. Its only flaws, he

* Although altered and no longer white, it still stands today four-square, with corner turrets, just as it did when it was first built. All around now lie other buildings, which have been added from time to time, and also a moat, now empty of water. The Tower was never needed to command or defend the City. It has, instead, served as a royal residence and a state prison. It has also housed at different times the Royal Mint, the Public Records, the Royal Observatory and an armoury. In 1256 Henry II kept his pet elephant there; Henry III kept both an elephant and a lion, and later, Henry VII kept a polar bear, which, tied to a long chain, was allowed to swim in the river each day, where it could catch fish to eat. From the days of the first elephant right up to the nineteenth century, a royal menagerie was always housed at the Tower, and, even today, it has its flock of pampered ravens. The Tower is now a showplace, open to the public. Two particularly interesting things among many to be seen there are the original Norman chapel, and the collection of Crown Jewels. The Tower was defended by its own soldiers, called the Yeomen of the Guard, who survive there today as showmen in curious old uniforms. They are often called Beefeaters, a nickname acquired after the Restoration of 1660 from an Italian traveller, who was impressed by the large daily rations of meat the guards were allowed.

† Of all the mediaeval buildings on the riverside, only the Tower, Westminster Abbey, parts of Lambeth Palace, the Great Hall of the Royal Palace at Westminster and Southwark Cathedral remain today.

A Norman ship.

thought, were that many foolish inhabitants were too often drunk, and that there were too many fires.

He tells us that London in his time had no less than 126 parish churches, and thirteen larger ones for monasteries and convents. These served a population of no more than about 50,000. 'To this City', wrote Fitzstephen, 'Merchants bring Wares by Ships from every Nation under Heaven. The Arabian sends his Gold, the Sabean his Frankincense and Spices, the Scythian Arms, Oil of Palms from the plentiful Wood; Babylon her fat Soil, and Nilus his precious Stone; the Seres send purple Garments; they and Norway and Russia Trouts, Furs and Sables; and the French their Wines.'

The good monk believed that 'a city should not only be commodious and serious, but also merry and sportful', and he described a sport which took place on the river at Easter-time. A shield was fixed to a pole in the middle of the river below the bridge, and in the prow of a boat which was driven along by the current stood a young man ready to charge the shield with a lance. If he hit the target, broke his lance and stayed upright, he scored a point, but if his lance did not break and he fell into the water, he lost a point. Then, wrote Fitzstephen, 'upon the bridge, wharfs and houses by the river's side, stand great numbers to see and laugh thereat'.

Here is proof that London had a bridge at this period. We also know from other sources that the bridge had been burned down in 1136 in one of London's bad fires, and that in 1163 it was rebuilt in elm under the direction of a priest called Peter Colechurch. That elm bridge was almost certainly the one mentioned by Fitzstephen.

Ever since Roman days, the bridge had been made of wood;

A drawing from an old print showing the sport on the river as described by the monk William Fitzstephen.

so it would rot in time, or be burned, and have to be rebuilt again and again, which was both a nuisance and an expense. Then in 1176 the rebuilding of London Bridge was begun in stone for the first time. It took thirty-three years to complete, and its construction was a great feat for its age. Again Peter Colechurch directed the building, and he did it well, for the Bridge lasted more than six hundred years.

At first it carried a road twenty feet wide and over three hundred yards long, supported by twenty arches, each curving to a point at the top in the Gothic manner. The arches varied in width, and this added to the rough charm of the whole. At one place no arch spanned the piers; instead there was a drawbridge of wood, which could be raised up against a tower when a tall ship wanted to pass upstream.

Around the bases of the piers were laid starlings. These were like long islands pointed at both ends, and they protected the bases of the piers against the strong and ceaseless flow of the river. They consisted of an outer wall of wooden stakes driven into the bed of the river, behind which rough stones had been thrown to displace the water.

These starlings held back the water, so that the Bridge resembled a long weir. When the tide turned, the fall of water below the arches was like a mill-race, and the fall could be as high as five feet. Through the centuries people often enjoyed the sport of shooting down this fall in small boats, although many were drowned that way.

In time, the force of water was used to turn water-wheels fixed below the arches at both ends of the Bridge—first for grinding corn, and later for pumping up water into the City from the river. The force of water was also useful in that it carved out a deep pool below the Bridge where large ships could float. Because the Bridge slowed down the flow of water, the river above the Bridge sometimes froze in cold winters, and then great carnivals would be held on the ice.

Soon after the Bridge was finished, houses were built on both sides, so that to cross the Bridge was like going along a narrow

Old London Bridge in the Middle Ages with its central chapel.

street. The houses jutted out over the river and were supported there by timbers sloping back to the stonework of the Bridge, but, even so, the width of the road between the houses was reduced to only twelve feet. The houses were often rebuilt through the centuries, and almost all were of timber framing, so that they would not be too heavy for the Bridge to bear. They became quite large, however, with several storeys, and they had shops at street level. Some were joined across the road on their upper floors by little bridges.

The Bridge was a pleasant place on which to live, for the houses had open views up and down the river, where something interesting was always happening. Ships arrived or sailed away, and between them numberless small craft were always on the move. And those who lived on the Bridge could let down a line into the river at any time and fish from their windows.

The Bridge was often noisy with the sounds of horses, carts, and cattle echoing between the walls of the houses, the roar of the water rushing below, and the squawking of the many scavenging kites and ravens, which were always flying around or perching upon the Bridge and its buildings.

As well as the dwellings and shops, a stone gateway was built across the Bridge towards the south end. On its roof long poles stood up against the sky, on which were stuck the rotting heads of

traitors as a warning to others who might be plotting against the King. Near the middle of the Bridge on the east side, a beautiful stone chapel with a croft below it projected into the river. It was dedicated to Thomas à Becket, the Martyr of Canterbury, who had been murdered in 1170 a few years before the Bridge was begun. He was a Londoner born and bred, was for a time Constable of the Tower and was always proud to sign himself 'Thomas of London'. He had been baptised in St Mary Colechurch where Peter Colechurch was a priest, and was much venerated, both in the City and in Southwark. Colechurch, who died three years before his bridge was finished, was buried in this chapel.

Old London Bridge played an important part in the history of the City, and so the City has often been called the Parasite of the Bridge. During the Middle Ages, it was the scene of many historical occasions, and also a number of fires. In 1212, for example, a disaster occurred when a crowd of people were trapped on the Bridge between two fires; many were burned to death in the crush, while others, who jumped into the river, or into boats which sank in the turmoil, were drowned. In the winter of 1282 came a long and terrible frost. When a sudden thaw set in, the pressure of the blocks of ice which formed against the Bridge carried away four arches, and they had to be rebuilt.

In 1216 Louis, eldest son of the King of France, crossed the

Bridge with an invading army, invited to England by the barons to help them in their rebellion against King John. In 1357 the Black Prince crossed in triumph after the Battle of Poitiers with his captives, King John of France and his son. There in 1381 Wat Tyler of Kent and his peasant mob, in revolt against the taxes, broke through to the City. There in 1396 passed a gorgeous procession, when Richard II brought to London his eight-year-old bride, Isabella, daughter of the French king; and there in 1415 Henry V was welcomed with joyful ceremony after his victory at Agincourt. On such great occasions, the Bridge would be richly decorated with coloured flags, tapestries and coats of arms, as though it were a triumphal entrance to the City.

What did the whole riverside and the City look like in these times—say to a young sailor on his first visit to London from the Continent in the year 1400, when Henry IV had been on the throne for a year?

Rounding the Isle of Dogs, his ship approaches the Tower, which, gleaming white in the morning sunshine, has been in sight for some time across the marshes. Away in the misty distance lie the wooded slopes which will one day be covered with the houses of Hampstead and Highgate. Behind the Tower rises the wonderful city of spires and bell-towers, dominated by the great cathedral of Old St Paul's on the top of the western hill, with its lead-covered spire soaring five hundred feet into the air, the highest in Christendom, and bearing on its top a ball, an eagle-cock, and a cross fifteen feet high, all covered with gold. With its aspiring and masterly church architecture, this London looks very different from the Roman *Londinium* whose skyline, with its low-pitched roofs, had been comparatively flat and dull.

The ship passes the Tower, where a strange fleet of long, elegant galleys is moored, each manned by 180 oarsmen and protected by a company of archers. The fleet has just arrived from Venice on its annual trading visit to London.

Soon the ship glides through a forest of masts, which rise from the throng of squat vessels anchored in the river, their 'castles' rising high, both fore and aft. Ahead stands the fabulous Bridge.

A drawing from a fifteenth-century wood-cut of mediaeval London, a city of churches and bell-towers.

Just before reaching it, the ship is steered gently to starboard, and, as the sail is lowered, it is tied up in a wide bay with cobbled sides. This is Billingsgate, one of the two main harbours of the City. The other one, Queenhithe, lies above the Bridge, and to reach it the

A drawing from a Flemish illumination of the late fifteenth century, now in the British Museum, showing, in an imaginary way, the Tower of London and, in the distance, Old London Bridge with its central chapel. This is the first known picture of the Bridge.

drawbridge must be raised, for which a fee of sixpence is charged.*

The smell is strong around Billingsgate, for it is a fish market.†

* About £1.50 in modern value.

† It is still London's chief fish market today.

A crowd of people has gathered to watch the ship arrive. Many talk in foreign languages, because in London live not only Englishmen, but Germans, Italians, Frenchmen, Scandinavians, and Flemings, who have settled in the city to trade. A wealthy merchant passes by with slow dignity, dressed in a velvet robe of purple lined with fur, with sleeves trailing to the ground, and wearing a coloured turban on his head and long pointed shoes on his feet.

As the sailor leaps ashore, he notices how the old defensive wall has decayed all along the river front. Street traders, including a water-seller, shout their wares around him, and he passes a rowdy group of young apprentices in short tunics, who should be learning their trades but have escaped for ten minutes into the freedom of the streets to play.

Plunging up a steep alley between timber warehouses, the sailor begins to explore the City. He finds it a rabbit-warren of narrow, crooked streets, over which the upper storeys of the houses project and sometimes nearly meet, so that neighbours up in the garrets can shake hands across the way. Streets are thus often dark; down their middles people throw their refuse, and there run gulleys which serve as open sewers. Whole families live, and sometimes also work, in single tenement rooms, and access to the upper floors in most of the houses is by outdoor staircases.

Many of the houses, roofed with thatch or wooden shingles, are of timber framing, the spaces between the timbers being filled with laths and plaster. But many houses are of stone—at least on the ground floors—for laws about building have long since been passed to try to reduce the frequent fires. Here and there, long poles with hooked ends can be seen lying along a wall, and others are available in every church; they are used to pull down thatch from any roof which may catch fire, and so stop the spreading of the flames.

A glance through open windows—few of which have glass in them or even translucent horn, but only shutters of matted wooden strips—reveals that the floors in most of the houses are covered with rushes. These make the rooms more cosy, but the rushes are rarely replaced with fresh ones, so that smells are often as bad indoors as out, and disease is spread by the filth and the fleas which collect in the rushes.

As he strolls along, the exploring sailor often comes to a refreshing open space: a market place, a wide stable yard, a churchyard, or a garden planted with herbs, vegetables, fruit trees and flowers around a monastery or the house of some wealthy merchant.*

He is surprised by the great number of parish churches, most of them built solidly of stone, and each with its tower and spire, pointed windows, buttresses, and carved decorations. A bell is always ringing somewhere close at hand, and other bells answer it farther off. Among the larger buildings are the taverns for travellers built around their courtyards, and the halls of the powerful Guilds, or City Companies—the Goldsmiths, Silversmiths, Vintners, Fishmongers, Mercers, and many others.

The sailor returns to Billingsgate and there he hires a boat from a waterman who will row him up river to Westminster and beyond. Before the boat passes through an arch of the Bridge—quietly enough, for the tide is at the slack—he sees on his right the famous church of St Magnus the Martyr, standing near the bridgehead.† Beyond the Bridge on the Southwark bank, rises the priory church of St Mary Overy with its tall square tower topped by pinnacles.‡ Beyond it stands the Palace of the Bishops of Winchester, with its

* On Chelsea Embankment, just west of Beaufort Street, can be seen today the great stone hall which formed the main part of the mansion of a wealthy London merchant of the fifteenth century. This is Crosby Hall, which was moved from Bishopsgate in the City for re-erection here at Chelsea in 1910 to form part of a new hostel for the British Federation of University Women. The hall was built in 1466 for Sir Richard Crosby, and is particularly interesting since it reveals in how grand a style an immensely rich wool stapler of London City lived during the Middle Ages.

† This was destroyed in the Great Fire of 1666, and was rebuilt by Sir Christopher Wren, whose building still exists today.

‡ After the Dissolution of the Monasteries by Henry VIII, St Mary Overy was called St Saviour's, and in 1905 it became Southwark Cathedral. Overy, or Over-ie, means over the water.

Crosby Hall today.

great hall and chapel, while, farther along the south bank, is the smaller Palace of the Bishops of Rochester.

Soon the boat is pulling past the Steelyard on the north bank, the imposing headquarters of the Hanseatic merchants, sometimes called Easterlings, who have monopolised the Baltic trade. All along the river front stands a tight jumble of wharves and warehouses, and at Queenhithe Harbour, sprouting a thicket of masts, the sailor looks up at the soaring spire of Old St Paul's. Where the City wall ends at the north-west corner stands Baynard's Castle, its dozen towers rising straight from the river. Beyond the Black Friars' Monastery, the sailor peers along the Fleet River, where coal-boats from Newcastle and many other vessels are floating all the way up to Holborn Bridge, and, from here to Westminster, the north bank, called the Strand, offers many pleasant sights. The first of these is the White Friars' Monastery and its grounds, and next come the buildings and gardens of the Knights Templar.*

After that follows one great rambling mansion after another, each with its private chapel, its great hall where the whole household dines, its snug privy parlour, and other rooms, stables and outhouses. Some of these mansions are set close to the river, others lie farther back behind lawns and gardens, which run down to low walls with carved gateways opening on to landing stages, where decorated barges float. They are the town houses of noblemen and of the powerful princes of the Church, who live here with many servants and friends when they visit London to attend the Court or Parliament at Westminster. On their far side runs a rough road called the King's Road which joins Westminster with the City, while beyond it lies open country.

* The Knights of the Temple belonged to a religious Order of soldiers founded at Jerusalem in 1118, in the time of the Crusades, to protect Christian pilgrims on their way from the coast to the Holy City, and also to fight the infidels. Their fine old church in London still exists as Temple Church, having been well restored after its damage by bombs in the Second World War. Tradition says that it was in the Temple gardens that the red and white roses were picked to start the brawl which led to the Wars of the Roses (1455 to 1485). In time to come lawyers settled here in a centre called Middle Temple, which was conveniently situated between Westminster, the centre of law, and the City, the centre of commerce.

The priory church of St Mary Overy by the Bridge at Southwark.

The main buildings of mediaeval Westminster. From left to right, St Stephen's Chapel, the Great Hall and the Abbey.

One of the last of the great houses is called Scotland Yard, and there the Scottish lords live when they come to town to pay their respects to the King.*

Soon the sailor lands at some river stairs at Westminster. This is now quite a large town, though not a city yet, because it has no cathedral of its own. Here he finds the King's Palace and its new Great Hall, with its magnificent hammer-beam roof, spanning seventy feet and carved with gilded angels, which was completed two years back for Richard II.† He will be impressed by the Abbey of stone with its flying buttresses, carved windows filled with brilliant stained glass, and its soaring, vaulted interior. This is not Edward the Confessor's building of Norman style, for that has been pulled down long ago, and the whole has been magnificently rebuilt in the full Gothic style by Henry III (1216 to 1272). Then he visits the circular Chapter House of the Abbey, which has been serving for some time past as the usual meeting place of Parliament, and, outside again, he notices, close to the river and east of

* In several hundred years to come its name will still remain as that of the world-famous police headquarters which will be built here. These have now been moved to a modern building in Victoria Street.

† When it was ready, the prodigal king, dressed in cloth of gold decorated with pearls and precious stones, celebrated a royal Christmas there, when 300 servitors bore to the tables 26 roasted oxen, 300 sheep, and fowls without number.

The Drawbridge Gate of old London Bridge, built in 1428 and pulled down in 1577. Above this gate the heads of traitors were exposed on poles. Based on a drawing by Gordon Home, author of 'Old London Bridge'.

the Abbey, a long, tall building of stone, with windows carved and pointed in the Gothic way; it is St Stephen's Chapel, rebuilt in about 1347 by Edward III.*

The visiting sailor now looks across the river, and there he can see the towers and battlements of Lambeth Palace, the town house of the Archbishop of Canterbury, which is well situated within easy ferry distance from Westminster. Continuing his journey up the river, he notices on his right the water-mill of the Abbot of Westminster, where the Tyburn stream is turning the great wheel.† Then he passes a windy, open space, very marshy but containing some market gardens, called Tothill Fields. At last he arrives at a hamlet with a little church called Calchythe, which means Chalk Wharf.‡

The boat swings round and is rowed back to Billingsgate, with the current to help it along at good speed. A small sailing craft, piled high with vegetables from Tothill Fields, sails past on its way to the City market, and then, gliding upstream, comes a stately barge, carved and painted and gilded, in which a noble lord reclines with his lady beneath a coloured canopy, while his servants chant a song in rhythm with their oars.

Now we can begin to see how the bones of modern London, inside its ever-swelling mound of flesh, were formed. There was the Bridge which made the city—the merchant's City itself behind its old defensive wall—the busy port on the river—the Tower on the south-east corner of the City, first built as a royal threat and conveniently linked by the river with the Royal Palace at Westminster—Southwark facing the City across the river around the south gateway of the Bridge—Westminster two miles up river,

* In 1547 the chapel ceased to be a place of worship, and was used instead as the debating chamber of Parliament. The debating chamber of the House of Commons in the twentieth century, as a result, still has a plan like that of a chapel of the later Middle Ages, and, whenever they pass the Speaker's Chair, Members of Parliament continue to bow their heads, as if to an altar.

† The river-front here is still called Millbank.

‡ Later the name became Chelsea.

A London lady of about A.D. 1400.

centre of the country's law and government, where the King often lived with his court, and which was often at odds with its rival, the City—and, running between the City and Westminster, the Strand with its riverside row of noble palaces and gardens.

As time passed and shipping grew, the port expanded down river, and the richer people moved west and north-west to live. So began the division of greater London into the East End, with its docks and all the storehouses, chandlers' shops, rope walks, and poor, crowded dwellings of those who lived by shipping and sea-faring—the West End, with its wealthier houses, luxury shops, and entertainments—the Square Mile of the independent merchant city in between—and Southwark to the south, which in time was to spread and spread to become South London.

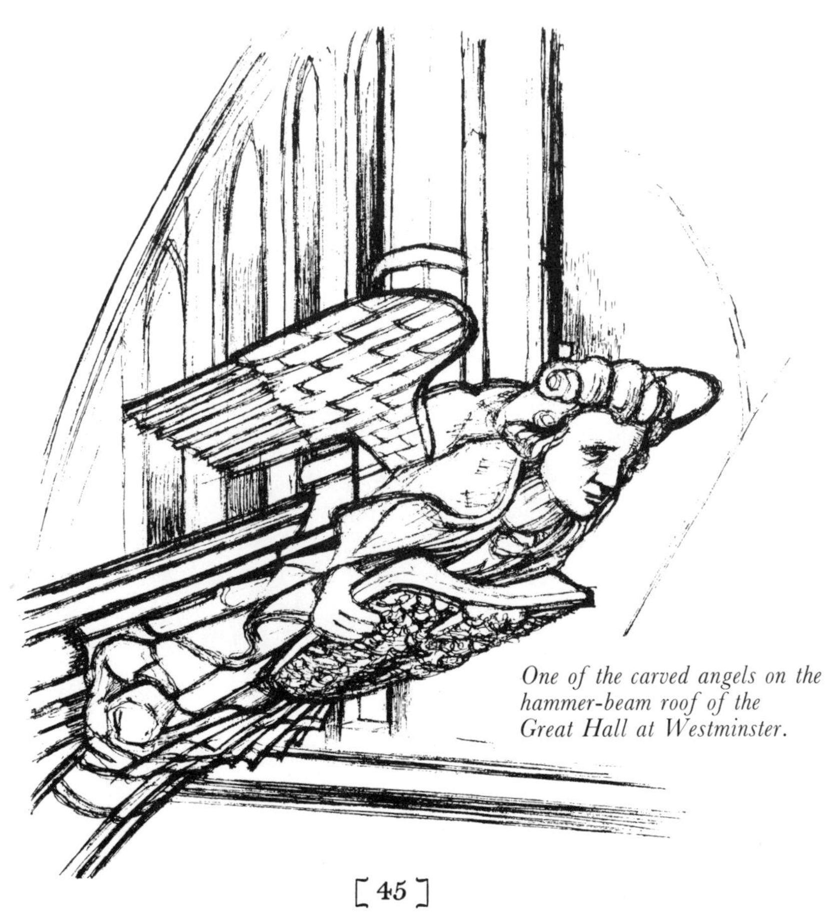

One of the carved angels on the hammer-beam roof of the Great Hall at Westminster.

CHAPTER V

Tudor Palaces and Pleasures

ALTHOUGH the City did not throw off its mediaeval, country-town look until it was rebuilt after the Great Fire of 1666, many changes came in the times of the Tudors. During the Middle Ages, the spread of the City beyond the wall on all sides had been checked by the large amount of land there which the monasteries owned. But when Henry VIII, in his struggle against the authority of the Roman Catholic Church, dissolved the monasteries and the monks were cast adrift in the 1530s, many new, secular buildings began to spread over those districts beyond the wall, which were called the Liberties. There was much speculation in property, and land often changed hands.

For some time after the Reformation few new churches were built, and the lead given to architecture passed from the Church to the nobility and middle classes. Wealthy peers, merchants, public servants and squires acquired Church properties confiscated by the King. They took over most of the large houses in and around the City which had formerly belonged to the Church, or they built fine new mansions on old Church lands.

They built them mostly of red brickwork, sometimes laid in patterns, and often as an infilling to a framework of oak, with rough decorations, many turrets and ranges of twisted chimneys of brick to serve the great open fireplaces inside. The ceilings of the rooms were richly decorated with moulded plasterwork, and the walls were either panelled in oak or hung with colourful tapestries. Windows grew ever larger as glass became cheaper, and they were often built in projecting bays.

Many of the big houses along the Strand were taken from the bishops and were sold or given away by the King, and some were rebuilt by their new owners. Henry VIII moved from the old

A Tudor ship.

royal palace close to the Abbey at Westminster, which was in decay, to another one close to the river, a little farther to the north. He had confiscated this from Cardinal Wolsey, who, before his quarrel with the King about his divorce from Katharine of Aragon, had been living there lavishly with eight hundred attendants. It was called York Place then, because it belonged to the Archbishopric of York, but changed its name to Whitehall.

Henry added more land and buildings to the property. On the far side of a long, wide courtyard with ornate archways at either end, where the street called Whitehall runs today, the King, who was fond of sport of all kinds, built tennis-courts, a bowling green, a tilt-yard for jousting with lances on horseback, and an eight-sided building for cock-fighting.*

The old palace with its Great Hall to the south near the Abbey was then used as the fixed centre of Parliament, and to this day the Houses of Parliament are still often called the Palace of Westminster.

Henry VIII built palaces everywhere. Just outside the City to the west of the Fleet River he built one with two wide courtyards, called Bridewell, where he could entertain foreign visitors of state. After the King's death, it was taken over by the City authorities for use as a House of Correction, where vagabonds and wrongdoers were held, forced to do hard labour and flogged at intervals.

Other big houses were built at the village of Chelsea along the river to the west, so that it came to be called the Village of Palaces. The gentle and learned Sir Thomas More built a comfortable, symmetrical mansion there, facing the river across a garden. About half a mile to the east of this Great More House, Henry VIII built another Chelsea palace, but he rarely stayed there himself and used it mainly as a royal nursery for his children. His wives, Catherine Parr and Anne of Cleves, both lived there for a time, and Anne died there.†

* Most of this Tudor palace was burned down in 1698, and all that is left of it today is the name Whitehall, and a large cellar where the King stored his wine. The cellar can still be seen, and is open to visitors at certain times.

† It was situated where Cheyne Walk runs today, about half-way along.

A drawing from part of the map of Agas made about 1570 which shows the palaces of the Strand lying between the City to the east and Westminster to the west. On the right is the Fleet River and on its bank Henry VIII's Bridewell Palace.

Facing the Isle of Dogs down the river at Greenwich, the King owned another palace, which he had inherited from his father. Like his daughters Mary and Elizabeth, he was born there, and in its chapel he married three of his wives. He loved the placc and greatly altered and enlarged it. Whenever Henry or his family were in residence at Greenwich Palace the Royal Standard would fly above the roofs, and every armed ship that passed on the river would fire a salute of cannon.

More and more ships sailed up and down the river past Greenwich in those Tudor times. They would arrive at the City with fine clothes, silks, carpets, timber, sugar, spices, wine, jewels, saltpetre for gunpowder, and, in Elizabeth's days, tobacco from Virginia. They would carry away woollen cloth, tin, hides and the leather garments of the fellmongers.

But ships sailed from London not only to carry English goods to foreign markets, but to explore the oceans of the world, to discover new sources of wealth and trade, and to found new colonies on distant shores. Many romantic companies of merchant adventurers were formed, the most famous being the East India Company, to which Queen Elizabeth granted a charter in 1600.

In the reign of Henry VIII ship-building yards were opened on the riverside below the Tower at Deptford and Woolwich, where hammering never ceased on the long galleons of the new navy, built to hold rows of iron cannon pointing through holes between decks. These cannon could be fired simultaneously in those broadsides which were revolutionising warfare at sea. The English navy helped to defend the merchant ships, and so enabled them to capture the trade routes of the world, not only in the North Sea, the Baltic and the Mediterranean, but now in the Atlantic to the west, and as far as the Indian Ocean to the East.

A spirit of adventure, strengthened by a new national confidence and pride, was in the air. In all the new, sea-going activities Londoners played a major part, and from London ships now sailed to every corner of the globe.

Very few pictures exist of mediaeval London, but the London and its river of these expansive Tudor times have been well recorded in two magnificent maps which have been preserved. They are not like the maps of today, which are drawn to scale, but more interesting, because they are like panoramic drawings.

The old Tudor palace by the river at Greenwich, facing the Isle of Dogs.

The first of them was made by Antony van den Wyngaerde at some time between 1543 and 1550, either at the end of Henry VIII's reign or during the short reign of the boy-king, Edward VI. It is ten feet long, and is at the Bodleian Library at Oxford. On it can be seen not only every building, but every ship on the river as far down as Greenwich Palace. It even shows how people dressed.

Large sailing ships are shown tied up in the harbours, anchored in mid-stream, or arriving and departing, and here and there a small sailing barge called a hoy is seen scudding along. A timber raft floats down stream, below Old St Paul's a state barge is being rowed along by eight oarsmen, and a horse-ferry is just leaving the south bank at Lambeth on its way across river to Westminster and Whitehall.*

The second map was drawn by Ralph Agas in about 1570, during the reign of Queen Elizabeth I. It is different in style, and less naturalistic, than Wyngaerde's panorama. Original copies of it, six feet long, can be seen at the Guildhall in London, and at Magdalen College, Oxford. It shows such lively details as a man bringing two horses down to the river to fill the barrels on their

* The telling Horseferry Road still runs down to the river at Westminster.

backs with water; some housewives are laying out their washing, and up at Moorgate, just outside the City wall on the north, some young men are practising with bows and arrows.

Agas also shows the river busy with ships and boats. At that time, thousands of watermen earned their living by rowing people across and along the river. Many of them were part-time smugglers, and because so much smuggling took place from newly arrived ships, a law was passed in Elizabeth's reign to compel all ships to unload under supervision only at certain legal quays. That made smuggling more difficult, but it went on all the same.

On both maps can be seen the buildings of Westminster. From the river there, some steps, just north of the Great Hall, lead up to an open place containing a conduit head covered with a dome. During public feasts, like coronations, that fountain would run red wine from France from its several spouts, which everyone could drink freely.

The old Abbey at Westminster, shown on both maps, had survived the Dissolution of the Monasteries because it had such close links with the monarchy. To the east end of the Abbey had been added Henry VII's chapel, with its magnificent and ornate fan-vaulting, the final flower of Gothic engineering in stone. For a few years the Abbey became a cathedral, and then Queen Elizabeth turned it into a church with an attached college.*

All around the public buildings of Westminster lay a few taverns and a jumble of small, squalid houses, where many lived in poverty—at least during the weeks when the Court was not in residence and trade was bad.

Westminster Abbey was a sanctuary. That is to say, it was a holy place, where evil-doers could find refuge from the Law. This sacred privilege had been granted to Westminster Abbey in Saxon days, and it continued for many years after the Reformation. Other sanctuaries existed at Whitefriars and in Southwark, but

* The college remains today as the famous Westminster School, where the boys still use some of the ancient monastery buildings. For the few years that the church was a cathedral, Westminster became a City. It is again a City today, because it contains the Roman Catholic Cathedral, completed in 1903.

Elizabethan dress.

they grew into such warrens of thieves, murderers and criminals of every sort that they were abolished towards the end of the seventeenth century.*

One difference between the two maps is that, while Wyngaerde's shows Old St Paul's with its great spire intact, Agas shows it without. That is because the spire was burnt down in 1561.

Another difference is that Agas shows Southwark to be more built up along the river than does Wyngaerde. Southwark, with its Bankside, had always been a resort of pleasure, and City people would often cross the Bridge or take a ferry to enjoy themselves there, even though it was full of pickpockets and other ruffians.†

The City authorities sometimes used Southwark as a place where they could dump, and so rid themselves of, low characters. But many Southwark people were law-abiding folk. Some ran local industries, especially tanneries by the river, where the necessary water was plentiful. Dyeing and weaving were also Southwark specialities, and so was printing; indeed, in 1536, under the patronage of St Thomas's Hospital, the first Bible in English was printed there.‡ Brewing was one of Southwark's main industries, because the area had always had many inns and eating-houses which brewed their own beer on the premises.

In Agas's map two round structures are shown, with un-roofed centres standing close to the river on the south bank. There noisy crowds watched cocks fighting and bulls and bears being baited. These so-called Wooden-Os were the first of the several theatres

* Sanctuary was regarded very seriously. In 1378, for example, Sir Alan Boxhull, the Constable of the Tower, with fifty armed followers, pursued two men who had escaped from the Tower and taken refuge in Westminster Abbey. Violating the Sanctuary, they killed one of the prisoners. This was considered so shocking that the Abbey was at once closed for four months.

† When they were caught, criminals would be locked up in one of the five Southwark prisons, perhaps in that damp, riverside dungeon called the Clink, a name still preserved locally in Clink Wharf and Clink Street. The word first meant a door-catch, and has now become a slang word for any prison.

‡ The first printing house in England was that of William Caxton, who set up his press next to the Chapter House of Westminster Abbey in 1470.

A drawing from part of the map of Wyngaerde made about 155
showing the City across the river from Southwark, and on the left
Bridge and St Saviour's Church, now Southwark Cathedral.

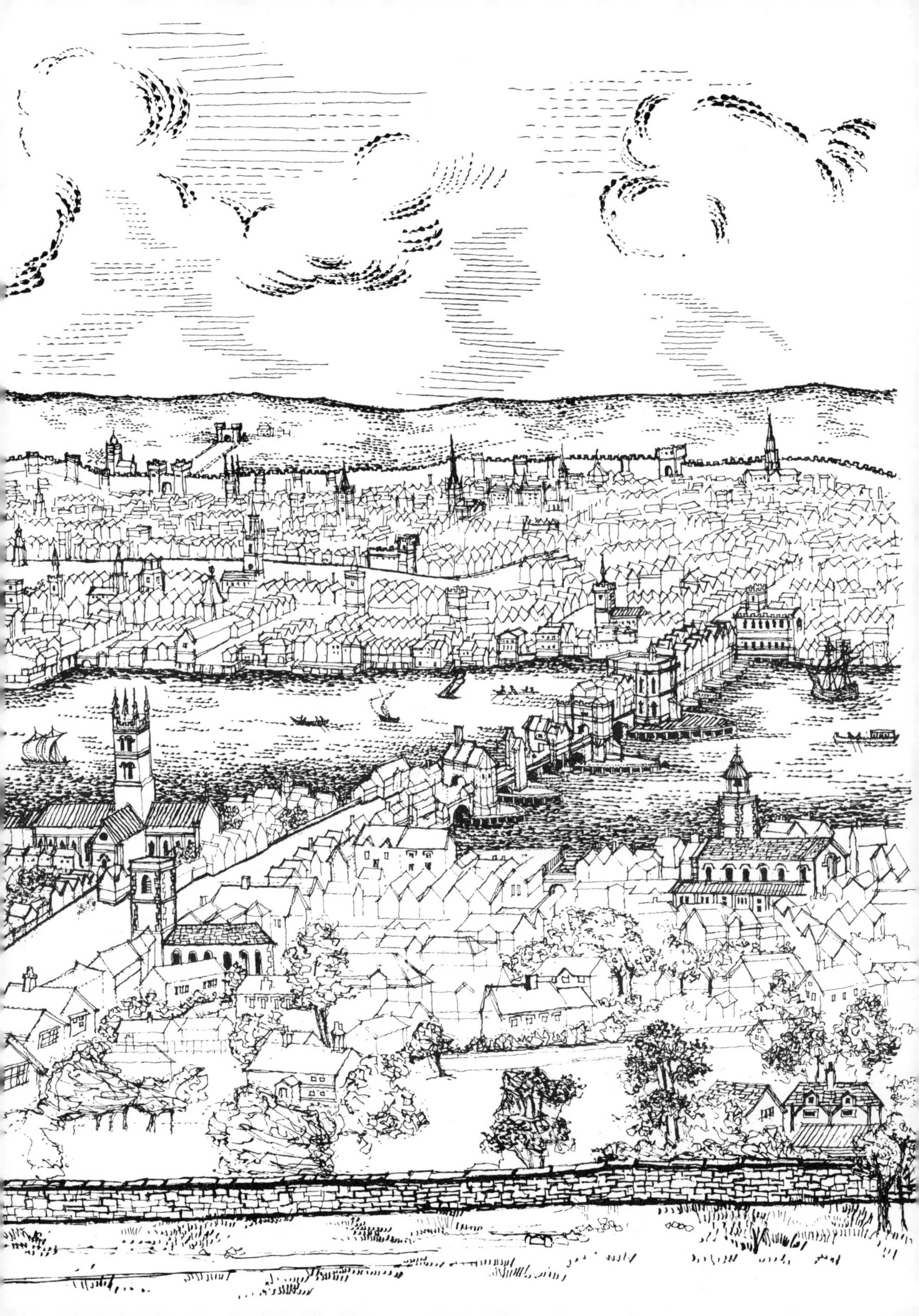

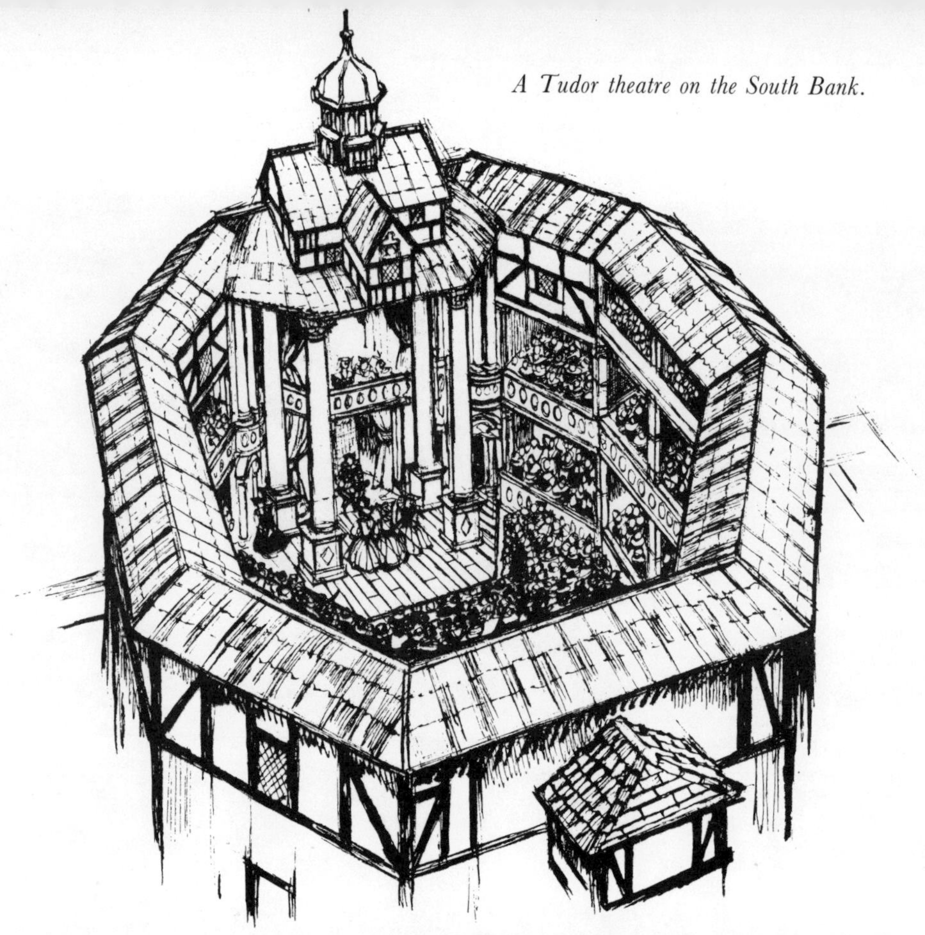

A Tudor theatre on the South Bank.

built in this area in Tudor times, for in some of them plays, as well as animal sports, were presented. Among them the Globe, built in 1598, became the most famous. It was of brick and timberwork, open to the sky at its centre, but surrounded with tiers of galleries around its sides, which were roofed.* There Shakespeare's plays were performed at a period when the English language blossomed gloriously in a brief Golden Age, and when Englishmen of every class were all in love with life.

When a play was to be presented, a flag would be flown high above the theatres, so that it could be seen from afar right across the river in the City. Trumpets sounded to announce that the play would soon begin—usually in the afternoon—and then people of every sort would cross the Bridge, or hurry down to the river steps

* As were the galleries around the courtyards of inns, which were, indeed, often used for play-acting.

to take the ferries and barges which would carry them across the river to enjoy some splendid new comedy or tragedy.

The animal sports in the Wooden-Os were cruel, but most people enjoyed them, not least Queen Elizabeth, who employed a Master of the Royal Game of Bears, Bulls and Mastiff Dogs. A foreign visitor described what he saw in the year 1598:

'The Bulls and Bears are fastened behind, and then worried by great English bull-dogs; but not without great risk to the dogs, from the horns of the one and the teeth of the other; and it sometimes happens they are killed upon the spot . . . To this entertainment there often follows that of whipping a blinded Bear, which is performed by five or six men, standing circularly with whips, which they exercise on him without mercy, as he cannot escape from them because of his chain; he defends himself with all his force and skill, throwing down all who come within his reach, and are not active enough to get out of it, and tearing the whips out of their hands and breaking them.'

Other amusements, less cruel, could be enjoyed in London. Everyone sang, played music and danced, and they talked abroad of the Dancing English. Fairs, like the annual Bartholomew and Southwark fairs, were held as much for revelry as for marketing, and there visitors could watch performing animals, puppet-shows, conjurors, tumblers, fire-eaters and jugglers. The Sovereign or the City Fathers would sometimes arrange vivid pageants on the river. One such was held three days before Elizabeth's coronation, when the Queen made a river journey from Whitehall down to the Tower, together with the Lord Mayor, Corporation, and leaders of the great City Companies. The Queen journeyed to the Tower on this occasion because it was the custom of the Tudors, as it had been of the Plantagenets, to reside there before their coronation at Westminster. Someone who was present described this procession, with 'their barges decked with banners of their crafts and mysteries, artillery shooting off lustily as they went, with great and pleasant melody of instruments, which played in a sweet and

The entrance to the Tudor palace of St James's.

heavenly manner.' The clothes were brilliant, the Mayor being robed in crimson velvet with a girdle of gold about him, and the aldermen being all in scarlet.

The Lord Mayor of London at this time held his annual procession on the river. He ranked next to the King in the City, but he had to receive the King's approval of his election. In 1453 began the custom of the Lord Mayor's journeying to Westminster by river to receive the royal assent, and this ceremony continued until 1856, when the procession took to the land and became the annual Lord Mayor's Show.

Such processions would pass under London Bridge when the tide was well in, and the rush of water under the arches had slackened. The old Bridge with all its buildings is clearly drawn on the maps of both Wyngaerde and Agas. But the wonderful Nonesuch House does not appear on either map, for that was not built until 1577 or later to replace the Drawbridge Tower. Stretching right across the Bridge, with a tunnel running through it at street level, Nonesuch House had a framework of timber parts which had been shipped from Holland, and not a single nail was used in its construction. The windows were large; at its corners were towers; the whole was painted and ornamented, and on its roof gilded weather vanes twirled and glinted. There a number of lords lived in grand style, for the Bridge had become very fashionable.

In the year 1580 the Bridge acquired a strange machine below an arch at its north end. This was the first of the wooden water-wheels, which, turned by the tide, could pump up water from the river into the City. It was invented by a Dutchman called Peter Morice and was most useful, because the drawing of water from the river by hand was hard, slow work. The pump worked well, and two years later Morice was allowed to build another wheel below the second arch of the Bridge.

An artist and map-maker called Norden made a drawing of the Bridge, including the water-wheels, at the end of the sixteenth century, and he described the Bridge as being 'adorned with sumptuous buildings, and statlie and beautiful houses on either side, inhabited by wealthy citizens and furnished with all manner

The splendid Nonesuch House, built with a timber framework about 1577 to replace the old Drawbridge Gate on London Bridge.

of trades comparable in itself to a little Citie'. Never before had the Bridge looked so fine. It was a fitting symbol for a vigorous and colourful age.

CHAPTER VI

Stuart Death and Rebirth

GREAT calamities and changes came to London and its riverside during the seventeenth century. It was an eventful period for the whole country, for in it occurred the union of England and Scotland under James I; the Civil War between Charles I and Parliament; the rule of Cromwell and the Commonwealth; the restoration of the monarchy under Charles II; the Great Plague and the Great Fire of London; the bloodless Glorious Revolution of 1688; and the founding of the National Debt in 1692 and the Bank of England two years later, both of which established the ever-growing financial power of the City.

In the first half of the century the growth of English colonies overseas, in the West Indies and America, and, as trading stations, in India, affected the shipping scene on London's river. From there many emigrants sailed away, some in the large, stately ships of the East India Company, on long hard voyages which could last for a year.

The splendid panorama etched by John Vischer in 1616 shows that London in the early seventeenth century looked very picturesque from a distance, with its many spires rising above the jumble of gabled roofs. But down in the alleys and courtyards, especially in the poor districts of the Liberties outside the wall, the City was very crowded and built-up.

People complained that England was like a man with rickets, with its head—the capital—too big for its body. Between 1603, when Elizabeth died, and 1660, when the Monarchy was restored —only 57 years—the population of the City, together with that of Westminster, the Liberties and surrounding parishes, rose from about 200,000 to over 400,000. By the end of the century, in spite of the Plague and the Fire, which slowed down London's growth

Even in Stuart times, before the Great Fire, the City was still largely mediaeval in appearance, with timber-framed houses and narrow alleys.

very little, it was over 600,000, and that in a national population of only about six millions.

Except during the rule of Cromwell, London was a gay town in many ways, but it was also dirty, unplanned and unhealthy. The rich lived well enough, but a wide gap existed between rich and poor, and whole families lived in single rooms, often in damp, dark cellars.

The air of London was so fouled by coal fires that smogs were even more frequent then than they are today, but nothing was done to reduce them, because the authorities did not want to discourage the burning of sea-coal, from the sale of which large taxes were raised. The alleys were narrow, filthy and unpaved. Water would spout and drip from the roofs on to those who passed by, long after

A drawing from part of the panorama made by Vischer in 1616 showing the City across the river from Southwark before the Great Fire.

At the top left is Old St Paul's Cathedral, without its spire, while at the bottom left are two of the South Bank theatres.

the rain had stopped. No proper drains existed to carry off either rainwater or sewage, and sewage often found its way into the streams and wells from which people drew their water.

Horses, coaches, and, after 1634, sedan chairs, crowded the streets. It is, therefore, not surprising that when they wanted to travel from one part of London to another, either on business or pleasure, most citizens preferred to use the fresh, open river—even if the wind there did often ruffle the great curly wigs which had become fashionable among men.

Some 40,000 watermen were rowing and sailing their wherries on the river between Windsor and Gravesend, and of them at least 3,000 were working between the City and Westminster. They served as the London taxi-drivers of those days, so that when horse coaches began to run for hire in the streets in 1565, they complained bitterly about this threat to their livelihood—without adequate cause, for, in fact, they were not greatly affected.

In contrast to the general squalor, an important and noble building was erected at Whitehall in 1622. It was the first modern building in England—modern, that is, for its time, for it was purely 'classical' in its design in the way Italian architecture had been for a long while, with its columns and other stonework details copied and adapted from the temples and public buildings of the Ancient Romans. At that period, other buildings in England were

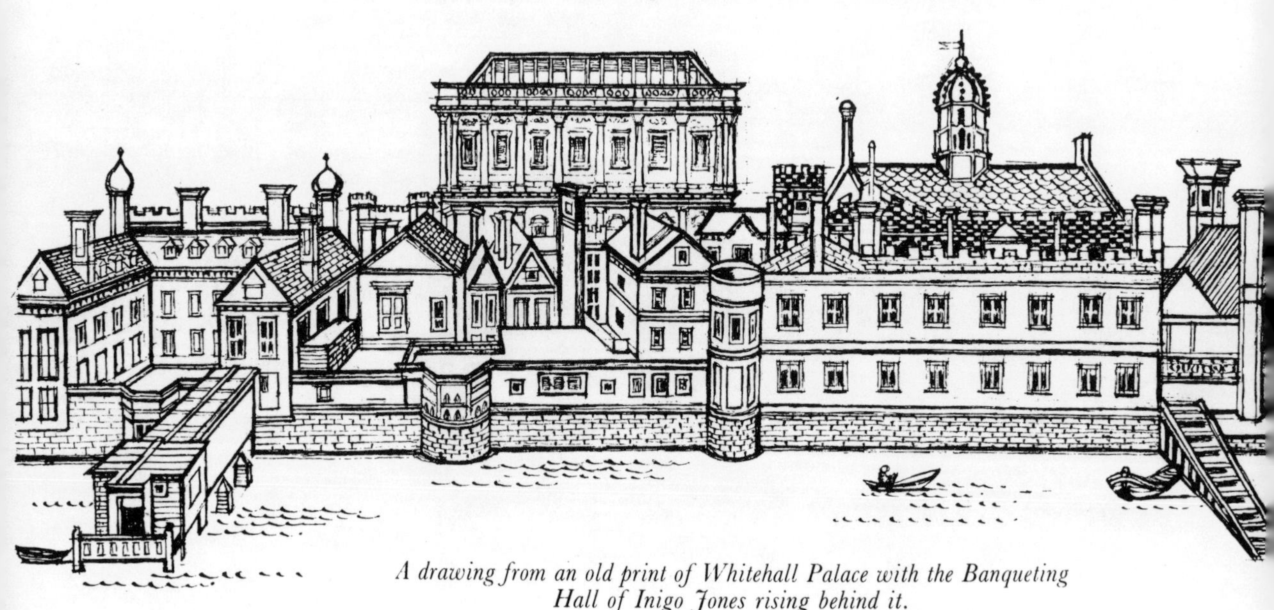

A drawing from an old print of Whitehall Palace with the Banqueting Hall of Inigo Jones rising behind it.

a muddled mixture of the old Gothic and new Classical styles, sometimes called 'Jacobethan', so that this new stone building seemed strange and very fine to Londoners.

It was designed by Inigo Jones, the London-born son of a poor Welsh cloth-worker, who twice visited Italy, where he learned much about the new style. He was a designer of stage scenery and of spectacular pageants called masques, and, as such, he was favoured by the King and his court. His calm, civilised facades, with their straight skylines, rows of pilasters and regular windows, must, indeed, have seemed more like theatrical scenery than a real building to most people in this chaotic, carpentered town of timber framing, brickwork, gabled roofs and carved barge-boards.

The building served as the royal Banqueting Hall, and was to form a small part of a huge, new classical palace of stone covering twenty-eight acres. The palace was never built, but the Banqueting Hall still stands in Whitehall today, although it cannot be seen from the river as it could in the past.

Another interesting building event occurred in London about thirty years after the Banqueting Hall was completed. Some of the Tudor houses at the north end of the Bridge were burned down in 1633 in a fire, which started when a maid-servant carelessly left a pail of hot ashes under a wooden staircase. The houses were then rebuilt in the new domestic style as regular terraces, three storeys high, and with dormered roofs. The Great Fire destroyed them, which was a pity, because they must have been a very pleasing group. As someone described them at the time they stood: 'Over about the houses were statlie platforms, leaded with rails and ballasters about them, very commodious and pleasant for walking and enjoying so fine a prospect up and down the river, and some had pretty little gardens with arbours.'

These houses survived during those middle years of the century which were disturbed by the Civil War. In that war London and its Bridge played an indirect but important part. Fighting began in 1642 between the armies of Charles I and Parliament, and in that year the Common Council of the City passed an Act 'for the better defence of the City by fortifying the same with outworks', and by closing most of the City gates. Earth ramparts to encircle London, Westminster and Southwark were dug by the militia helped by thousands of volunteers, although in the end they were not needed.

Most Londoners sided with Parliament, for, like the other seaports of England, the City was proud of the country's maritime skill and power, and it did not love the Stuart kings. It had not forgotten James I's neglect of the Navy, nor his execution of their hero Raleigh to please Spain, nor the attempts of Charles I to impose illegal taxes. In any case, the City had its own government and tradition of independence; since the Conqueror's time it had never been strongly royalist, and regarded Westminster as a rival.

The Londoners' support of Parliament was important in the war, because London not only controlled the lowest crossing of the dividing Thames, but formed both a wealthy supply base and a large recruiting centre. What is more, Parliament was able, as the King was not, to raise loans and impose taxes in the City, and with them it could equip its New Model Army.

Parliament won the war, and on January 30th, 1649, Charles I was executed on a platform outside the Whitehall Banqueting Hall. The monarchy and the House of Lords were both abolished, and a Commonwealth was formed. In 1653, Oliver Cromwell, who had been a successful general in the fighting and had become one of the Parliamentary leaders, installed himself in Whitehall Palace and ruled England as Lord Protector.

Londoners had a dull time under Cromwell. The Puritans believed that all pleasure was sinful; they closed the theatres, forbade dancing and singing, and even banned the revels of May Day and Christmas. The Globe Theatre was pulled down in 1644, and tenement houses were built on the site. Another famous theatre, the Hope, which stood near the Globe, and which was used for both plays and animal-baiting, survived until 1656, when all the bears, by command of the High Sheriff of Surrey, were shot to death by a company of soldiers.

Cromwell died in 1658, and eighteen months later, on May 29th, 1660, King Charles II was welcomed home to London from his long exile on the Continent. Although they had supported the Commonwealth, Londoners received this day with joy and excitement, and that it happened to be the King's birthday made an extra reason for celebration.

Led by the King, who was wearing a wide feathered hat above a great black wig of falling curls and riding a magnificent white horse, an endless, colourful procession crossed the Bridge, now richly decorated with banners and coats of arms. John Evelyn, who, unlike the other famous diarist of the period, Samuel Pepys, had always been a firm royalist, saw it all, and wrote:

'With a triumph of above 20,000 horse and foot, brandishing their swords and shouting with inexpressible joy; the ways strewed with flowers, the bells ringing, the streets hung with tapestries, fountains running with wine; the Mayor, Aldermen, and all the Companies, in their liveries, chains of gold, and velvet; the windows and balconies all set with ladies; trumpets, music, and myriads of people flocking, even so far as from Rochester, so as they were seven hours in passing the city, even from two in the afternoon till nine at night . . . nor so joyful a day and so bright ever seen in this nation . . . I stood in the Strand and beheld it and bless'd God.'

Livelier times returned to London after the Restoration. Charles II enjoyed life in his cynical, humorous way and loved music, dancing, feasting and theatre-going. Many people, especially his courtiers, imitated his pleasures, so that when the Great Plague smote London righteous men believed that God had delivered a just punishment for dissolute living.

Londoners lived in fear of disease of many kinds, especially smallpox and plague. Although no one knew it then, plague—or the Pestilence, as it was often called—was carried by black rats brought in ships from abroad, and the germs were then spread to human beings by fleas which had sucked the rats' blood. During the first half of the century plague in London was as frequent as it had ever been. In 1603, for example, some 30,000 died from it. In

Man's dress at the time of the Restoration.

Londoners flee to the country from the Plague. in 1630. From a contemporary broadsheet.

1625 even more died. There was a slighter attack in 1636, and then in 1665 came the Great Plague, which killed 100,000. It was a return of the Black Death, which had ravaged Europe 300 years before.*

Early in the hot summer of 1665 the sickness started in the suburban parish of St Giles-in-the-Fields. It spread quickly. As the death-roll mounted, more and more people fled from London or stayed indoors until hardly a soul could be seen in the streets, except those who were carting away the dead to the burial pits, ringing their handbells and endlessly intoning: 'Bring out your dead—Bring out your dead'.

On the river all movement ceased. The whole city seemed to be dying. The horror grew, and seemed to have no end. Month after month went by, and, as late as September 20th, Samuel Pepys, who had stayed in London to carry on his work as Secretary to the Navy, wrote in his Diary: 'But, Lord! what a sad time it is to see no boats upon the river, and grass grows all up and down White Hall court, and nobody but poor wretches in the streets!'

* This was the last serious epidemic in London until cholera and typhus came to the slums of the nineteenth century. One reason for this was that much of the rebuilding after the Fire was in brick and stone, instead of the old lath and plaster which made hidden spaces where rats could live. Another was the replacing of rushes on the floors with carpets and other materials, and of hangings and tapestries on the walls with panelling and plaster, for rushes and hangings harboured fleas. A third reason, and perhaps the main one, was that brown rats were killing off the black ones, and brown rats carried fewer plague-fleas.

Many of the watermen had moved up river to the open country, there to live in huts or tents on the banks. Down the river, ships lay in still rows in mid-stream, where they served as refuges for many frightened London families.

As the autumn advanced and colder weather came, the plague took fewer and fewer victims. Citizens who had fled trickled home from their country retreats and London began to revive.

Less than a year later, on September 2nd, 1666, came the second catastrophe. Although this one lasted for only four days and only six people died, it was the worst calamity London's fabric had suffered since Boudicca's raid in Roman times.

The Fire started late in the evening in a bakery in Pudding Lane, not far from the approach to the Bridge.* Standing in his nightshirt at the window of an inn on Bankside in Southwark, Pepys watched the fire spread. Later he wrote in his Diary:

* The spot is now marked by the column of the Monument.

The Great Fire of London seen from Southwark, with Old St Paul's being devoured by the flames.

'As it grew darker, appeared more and more, and in corners and upon steeples, and between churches and houses, as far as we could see up the hill to the City, in a most horrid malicious and bloody flame . . . one entire arch of fire from this to the other side of the bridge, and in a bow up the hill for an arch of above a mile long; it made me weep to see it.'

The next day the whole City was blazing. John Evelyn also watched from Bankside, and described what he saw:

'God grant that mine eyes may never behold the like, who now saw above 10,000 houses all in one flame! The noise and cracking and thunder of the impetuous flames, the shrieking of women and children, the hurry of people, the fall of towers, houses and churches, was like a hideous storm; and the air all about so hot and inflamed, that at the last one was not able to approach it, so that they were forced to stand still, and let the flames burn on, which they did, for near two miles in length and one in breadth. The clouds also of smoke were dismal, and reached, upon computation, near fifty miles in length. Thus, I left it this afternoon burning, a resemblance of Sodom, or the last day . . . London was, but it is no more!'

When the flames at last died down, it was found that four-fifths of the old City within the wall—that is some four hundred acres—were in smouldering ruins. 13,000 houses had been destroyed, together with eighty-eight churches, most of the halls of the City Companies, and even Old St Paul's Cathedral on the hill, which had been under repair and surrounded by inflammable timber scaffolding.

As soon as they had recovered from their first shock, the citizens faced their troubles well. The Liberties outside the wall were barely harmed—luckily enough, for here at least half the population of London lived. Some of the homeless set up tents at once in the suburbs, and, before long, most were living in close quarters with friends, relatives, and neighbours in the houses around the devastation.

What was to be done with the ruins? Several complete plans with new, wide, straight streets, and a riverside embankment, were at once drawn up by different men. Nothing came of any of them, mainly because so many people and businesses owned small pieces of land in the City, and would not sell them or agree to adjustments. The lack of enough money to buy the land for public use and rebuilding on a general plan was the chief difficulty—just as it has too often been in our own times. Thus, much of the ancient rabbit-warren of the City was re-created, and many of the roads, lanes and passages in the City have remained with us since mediaeval times.

Rebuilding was rapid and carried out under new laws, so that the city would at least be healthier, more comfortable, and less inflammable than it had been. Houses now had to be of brick or stone, the thicknesses of walls and heights of rooms were fixed, and pedestrians were protected by gutters from rainwater running down the roofs. A few large, general improvements were made too, and some streets were widened, especially by the river. The old slums around the City wall, however, remained for a long time after the Fire.

One of Wren's new London buildings erected after the Fire—the Customs House just west of the Tower. This no longer exists and another Customs House stands on the site.

Dr Wren, a mathematician, astronomer and architectural genius, later to be knighted as Sir Christopher Wren, had been among those who had drawn up plans for the City, and he was one of the men who guided its rebuilding. He designed many of the new City churches, as well as the new Cathedral of St Paul's, using that fine white Portland stone which is still typical of the monumental buildings of central London.

Within only five years of the Fire, much of the rebuilding of the City had been completed. The new houses were still close together, but the old squalor had gone. In the place of the confused jumble of timber-framed buildings stood many trim rows of brick and stone houses with regular casement windows. The doorways were charming, with their classical pilasters and decorations of carved wood or stone.

At the end of the century, the appearance of the new City from the river would have been unrecognisable to anyone who had known the place before the Fire and had suddenly returned from abroad. The sight would have thrilled him, for it was far more elegant and attractive than it had been. St Paul's, with its great swelling dome, rose high above the roofs of red tiles, and the whole skyline was broken by the steeples and towers of Portland stone, gleaming white and topped by glinting weather-vanes of gold, of Wren's fifty-one new parish churches. Each was different in form from the others, and all were beautiful.

Wren also designed other buildings in and around London. One was the new Customs House to the west of the Tower, which has since been replaced by a later building. Another was the famous hospital for old and wounded soldiers, which arose in the pastures to the east of Chelsea, a fine symmetrical building of stone and red brick, which is there today, and is still used for its first purpose.

Naval seamen also obtained their haven by the riverside. At Greenwich, Anne of Denmark, wife of James I, had had a house built behind the old palace to the design of Inigo Jones. It was in the new classical manner, a simple, dignified building of stone, not very large or grand. Charles II had the old Tudor palace on the riverside pulled down and began building a new one in its place.

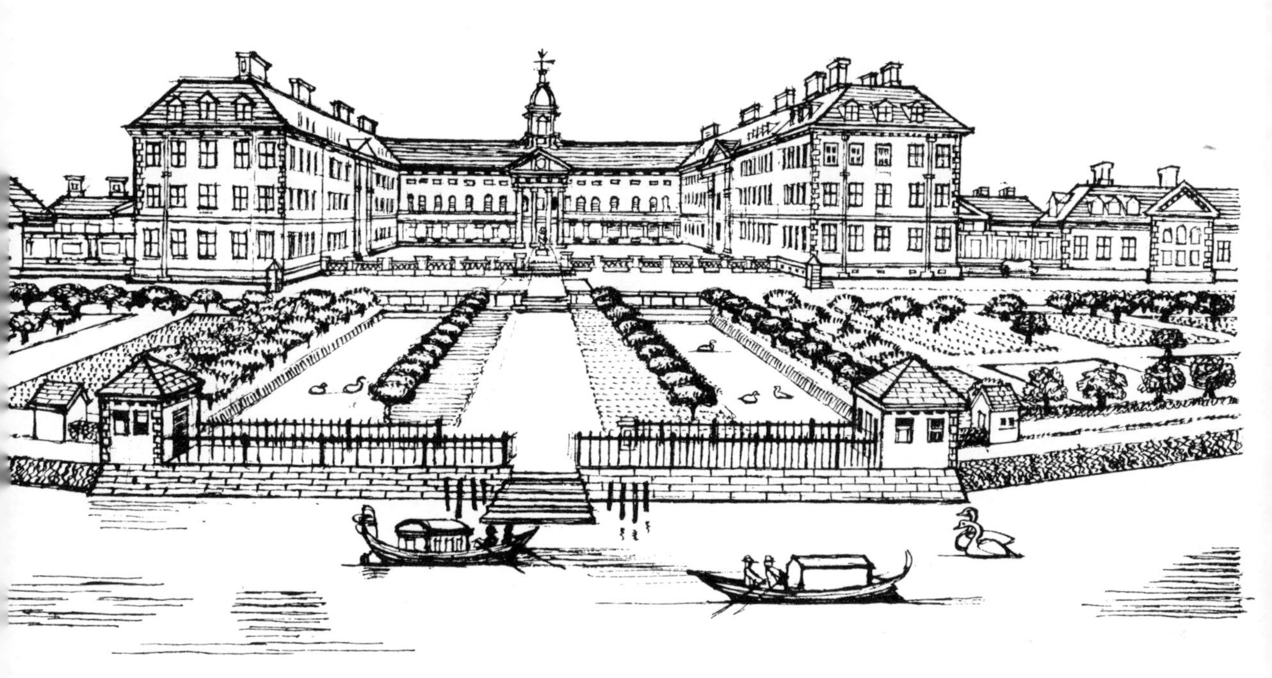

Another of Wren's riverside buildings—the Royal Hospital at Chelsea for retired and wounded soldiers. The building still stands, but the decorative ponds in the grounds and the look-out houses by the river which are shown in this drawing from an old print have gone.

That was not finished until well into the next century, and then not as a royal palace, but as an asylum for retired or wounded naval seamen. When complete, it was a monumental affair, with the small Queen's House far back on the axis. Wren had a major hand in its design, but other architects also worked on it.*

Most of the houses on the Bridge were saved from the Fire. Westminster, Whitehall, the Strand, the Liberties and Southwark were not touched by it, but Southwark suffered a serious fire of its own in 1676, when several of the old inns were destroyed, including the *Tabard*, from which Chaucer's pilgrims had, according to *The Canterbury Tales*, started on their journey. Whitehall also had its

* The whole is still there today, but is not used for its original purpose. The Queen's House is now part of the National Maritime Museum, while the rest, with its long colonnades, two domed towers, wings, and courtyards, is used as a naval college. The banqueting hall, with its impressive mural paintings, is particularly worth seeing.

Greenwich Hospital, built on the site of Greenwich Palace for retired and wounded seamen, as it appears today. Several architects worked on this grand scheme, including Wren. In the foreground is the Queen's House which became part of the scheme.

own fire in 1698, and this destroyed the Tudor palace.*

The Strand changed much after the Fire. It lost its high tone as a row of noble mansions set in formal gardens running down to river walls, for many of the owners sold their properties here to speculators, who built small houses and shops on the land. By the

* Wren made drawings for a new palace at Whitehall, in which the Banqueting Hall by Inigo Jones, having survived the fire, was to form the central feature. Nothing came of the scheme, for William III, who was asthmatic, preferred to live in the cleaner air of Hampton Court Palace, which lay miles up river. The official residence of the English sovereigns, however, became St James's Palace from the reign of William III until the accession of Queen Victoria in 1837. After that it was Buckingham Palace.

end of the century, most of the big houses had been pulled down, and the area was covered with new streets. Down by the river stood new wharves and warehouses for brewers, timber merchants and others. So London lost one of its world-famous sights, and few open spaces now remained along the riverside where Londoners could stroll and enjoy wide views.

By the end of the century trade and shipping were booming, and down river a number of new docks, both wet and dry, had been dug into the river banks, although they were neither enclosed, nor did they have lock entrances, like the docks that were to be built in the nineteenth century. The East India Company had built its own refitting dock at Blackwall as early as 1614, and in 1696 Howland's wet dock was dug at Rotherhithe, and remained London's largest dock for more than a century. It was a ten-acre lake, surrounded by rows of poplar trees to strengthen the banks, while at its end stood the mansion of the Howland family. In time it was used mainly for whaling ships until it was absorbed into the Surrey Commercial Docks, which are now mostly used for timber imports. In 1699 Billingsgate ceased to be a harbour, and became simply a fish market with stalls around the bay.

The river was still full of fish and fairly clean and clear, except after a storm. Then the water became so thick with mud washed down from the banks and along the streams, that fish could not see where they were swimming. At such times, fat haddock could be lifted straight out of the river below the Bridge by anyone who cared to dip a hand into the water.

The river was as lively and colourful as ever, and now a few pretty yachts, richly carved and gilded, were added to the many other craft afloat, for, among his pleasures, Charles II enjoyed yacht-racing, and had made the sport popular with the wealthy.

Let a festive note end this chapter of changes and calamities with an eye-witness account of one of those historic Frost Fairs, which took place on the river when it froze in hard winters. It comes from Evelyn's Diary, in entries made during the great frost which began at Christmas in 1683 and lasted until February of the next year.

A corner of the Howland Dock at Rotherhithe.

'I went across the Thames on the ice, now become so thick as to bear not only streets of booths, in which they roasted meat, and had divers shops of wares, quite across as in a town, but coaches, carts and horses passed over . . .

'The frost continuing more and more severe, the Thames before London was still planted with booths in formal streets, all sorts of trades and shops furnished and full of commodities, even to a printing-press, where the people and ladies took a fancy to have their names printed, and the day and year set down when printed on the Thames: this humour took so universally, that it was estimated the printer gained £5 a day, for printing a line only, at

A Frost Fair held on the Thames in Charles II's time, with its 'street' of booths and carriages passing across the ice—'a carnival on the water'. In the distance is the Bridge, which helped the ice to form in cold winters by holding back the flow of the river.

sixpence a name, besides what he got by ballads, etc. Coaches plied from Westminster to the Temple, and from several other stairs to and fro, as in the streets, sleds, sliding with skates, a bull-baiting, horse and coach-races, puppet-plays, and interludes, cooks, tippling, and other lewd places, so that it seemed to be a bacchanalian triumph, or carnival on the water.'

A pleasure yacht of Charles II's time.

CHAPTER VII

Georgian Growth and Gardens

CHANGES in England and its capital were slow during the first half of the eighteenth century, but around the mid-century there began that process of division between the old world of handicrafts and farming and the new world of the Industrial Revolution—the world of factories, machines and squalid, ever-spreading towns in which we still live today.

Wars, which increased the Empire, were fought throughout the century, culminating in 1815 with the Battle of Waterloo. They were fought abroad by small, professional armies and navies, and life at home was calm enough. During this century, and for three decades beyond, England reached its highest peak of culture—at least among the privileged few—and London was its teeming centre.

It was an age of violent contrasts—of luxury and squalor, of elegance and brutality, of degrading toil for the poor and elevating leisure for the rich. Parliament was mainly a rule of wealthy landlords, and poverty was taken for granted. Underfed children were put to ceaseless work in the new mines and factories, while more and more laws were made to bring wrong-doers to gruesome public death on the scaffold, where even children could be hanged for stealing. The soldiers and seamen on whom the country depended for its safety and prosperity were poorly fed and disciplined by constant flogging. Indeed, conditions were so bad in the royal ships that few men would join them voluntarily, and Press Gangs roamed the streets of London's riverside and other ports to capture men by force, and carry them off to a hard and dangerous life at sea.

The Royal Court in London was no longer the centre of fashion, learning, patronage and the arts, as it had been before, and the

A private soldier in the Grenadier Guards of 1792.

A merchant ship of the early eighteenth century.

lead in these things passed to the landed aristrocracy, who built fine houses on their country estates, filled them with works of art, and surrounded them with beautiful parks. Many owned London houses and estates as well.

The population of England and Wales rose from about six millions at the start of the century to nine-and-a-half millions at its close, while the population of greater London grew from about 674,000 in 1700 to 960,000 in 1801. So London contained about a tenth of all the country's inhabitants. Bristol and Norwich were the towns next in importance to London, and yet London held at least fifteen times the population of either. Even when manufactures developed in the Midlands and the North, and the new canals centred at Birmingham during the latter part of the century, London did not lose its powerful position, for its river was firmly linked with the country's network of waterways by the Grand Junction Canal.

The City merchants controlled a large proportion of all the country's business, and London's river grew ever more crowded with ships as trade developed with the growth of industries and Empire. Greater London, however, was not only the centre of trade, but also of the finest craftsmanship, of law, government, fashion, and all the arts, and it was more important now in every way as England's hub than it had ever been before, or was to be in the future.

Nearly half the English exports consisted of cloth woven from home-grown wool and imported cotton and silk, but imports were very varied. The colonists sent back raw materials like pig-iron, cotton, saltpetre and timber—the last very important for building houses and ships since England had cut down so many of her woods. From the eastern Mediterranean came Turkey carpets and large supplies of currants, while from the West Indies came sugar, chocolate and rum.

The East India trade was considerable, and London monopolised it. It brought spices, tea, cottons, silks and exquisite Chinese porcelain. The beautiful imports from the Orient had the effect of refining English taste in clothes, household goods, and even

A Georgian doorway with its fanlight.

Man's costume of the 1750s.

architecture, and so they added to the high culture of the times. They also stimulated handicrafts in England, like the hand-painted chinaware from such works as Bow and Chelsea. Less civilised activities went on too; in 1771, for example, as many as fifty-eight slave ships sailed from London during the year.

The East India trade also changed drinking habits, especially in the capital. There, during the first half of the century, cheap gin had replaced ale as the drink of the poor. It was their quickest escape from boredom and misery, and it killed them in thousands, until in mid-century the government at last placed a high tax on it and controlled its sale. The habit then decreased, and, by the end of the reign of George III, nearly everyone was drinking imported tea, often sweetened with sugar from the West Indies, though the upper classes also drank much imported wine.

Chocolate and coffee were popular drinks too. Coffee, indeed, had been so since the Restoration, at least among the upper and middle classes. In London the coffee houses were important social centres, where men could gather to read the news over their cups, or talk about politics or business. In Queen Anne's time London had at least five hundred such coffee houses. There people of different classes could mingle, much as they do in the pubs today, and in two such places were born London's Stock Exchange and the great shipping-insurance firm of Lloyd's. In time the gentry formed their own exclusive clubs in the West End, which, for them, came to take the place of the coffee houses. There they could dine, wine, talk politics, and gamble whole fortunes away.

London people were of all sorts. At the bottom of the scale were the thieves, pickpockets and other criminals. Then came the poor, unskilled labourers who lived mainly in the East End, Southwark and the suburbs, in slummy, overcrowded conditions. There were the merchants and the bankers, who lived with their families over their counting houses in the old City. There were the shop-keepers, with their homes on the floors above their elegantly decorated showrooms, which would be brightly lit at night by candles in hanging chandeliers and silver candlesticks to attract passing customers. There were the skilled craftsmen, the middle-

Lady's costume of the 1750s.

men—brokers, clerks and foremen—and the professional men, such as the lawyers in the Temple. In the West End lived the courtiers, politicians, noblemen and upper middle classes, attended by many servants—some of them in large mansions in their own grounds, and others in pleasant brick houses with projecting cornices, carved and hooded doorways, decorative ironwork, and the new, sliding, sash windows, which had begun to replace hinged casements at the start of the century. Most of these houses were joined together in terraces, and were often laid out in those charming squares with central, tree-filled gardens which, though now sadly mutilated, are with us still—Bloomsbury, Bedford, Russell, Fitzroy, Cavendish and others, built on land owned by noblemen, from whom most of the squares acquired their names.

Along the streets of the West End went the carriages of the gentry, which became ever more varied and graceful in their forms. On the new pavements might pass a sedan chair borne by two men, its roof raised so that the tall wig of the lady sitting within could protrude in comfort. Her skirt would be embroidered and hooped at the sides, and, the weather being warm, she might carry a

Hanover Square—a typical eighteenth-century London arrangement of new houses.

delicately-painted fan. The gentleman walking by her side would also wear a wig powdered white, and a three-cornered hat of black felt. His waistcoat, under a tail coat of velvet, would be embroidered with flowers, and below this he would wear knickerbockers, white stockings and buckled shoes, while an elegant sword would hang by his side.

Daniel Defoe, the London-born author of *Robinson Crusoe*, was a great reporter, and recorded what he saw of the country and its capital during the reign of George I in a book called *A Tour Through the Whole Island of Great Britain.* On London's river he found 'about two thousand sail of all sorts, not reckoning barges, lighters or pleasure boats and yachts'. From the Pool, just below the Bridge, down to Blackwall, he counted three wet docks for laying up ships, twenty-two dry docks for repairs, and thirty-three yards for building merchant ships. Southwark had become built up along the riverside like 'a long street of about nine miles in length reaching from Vauxhall to London Bridge and from the Bridge to Deptford, all up to Deptford bridge, which parts it from Greenwich, all the way winding and turning as the river winds and turns'.

On the north bank, a few miles west of Westminster, lay Chelsea, which was considered to be a very healthy place to live. Defoe called it a Town of Palaces, which 'by its new extended buildings seems to promise itself to be made one time or other a part of London, I mean London in its new extended capacity'. He added: 'If it should so happen, what a monster must London be.'

Far to the east, on the north bank beyond the Tower, the houses were densely built up in a strip stretching all the way from Wapping to Limehouse, and there lived seamen when they came ashore, and all those who supplied ships with ropes, sails, stores, and other needs. Here stood many taverns with balconies overhanging the river, where sailors met to drink, to exchange yarns of their adventures, to argue about the rig of some strange new ship which had just cast anchor in the river, or to collect a crew for another voyage.

All along this reach smuggling was rife, and many taverns had

The hanging of a pirate at Execution Dock in Wapping.
Redrawn from an old print.

their secret rooms in loft or cellar where the smuggled tea, rum, tobacco, and other goods could be stored until they were sold. As the river grew more and more congested, smuggling became easier.

It was well organised, and the general public did not regard it as a serious offence. Of the thirteen million pounds of tea consumed in the country during 1784, for instance, only five-and-a-half millions had paid duty.

Not enough warehouses existed where goods could be stored, and this led to much pilfering on the open quays. But early in the century, for the first time, some special warehouses were built, where imports like tea, coffee and chocolate could be kept 'in bond'; that is to say, duty did not have to be paid until they had been sold. The only port authority which controlled shipping and docking was the City of London itself, and it gained much profit from its charges.

This was an age not only of smugglers, but also of pirates. When caught at sea by naval ships, they would be brought to London for trial, and, if found guilty, they would be taken to Execution Dock on the riverside and hanged on a gibbet at low water. There the corpses swung for all to see, until three tides had flowed over them.

Big ships came no higher now than the Bridge, for its drawbridge was no longer raised. But at the Pool they clustered thickly, and far down river. Both below the Bridge and above it, small boats, rafts and barges moved continually, and some barges served as ferries, which could take carriages and horses across the river. Along the north bank between the Bridge and Westminster at least thirty landing places, with their stairs and piers, projected into the river.

Let us now look, in their order of appearance, at a few of the more important or curious structures which appeared on, near, or beside the river in the eighteenth century.

In 1724 the Chelsea Waterworks were founded near the Royal Hospital. They had a reservoir at the place where Victoria Station lies now. The water was pumped up from the Thames and from the Westbourne by the early, and very crude, steam engine invented by Newcomen. This great, clumsy affair was regarded as a curiosity, and people flocked to watch it wheezing and puffing at its wet and heavy work.

Another pump of this kind was set up in 1726, right on the river-front below the Strand. This also pumped water from the river, and supplied the York Buildings Waterworks, which had existed here since 1675, when the Strand gardens were being built over. A tall, tapering tower marked the spot, and beside it rose two iron chimneys to take away the smoke from the engine's fire.*

As a result of the growing size and population of London, the single old Bridge serving the City had formed a serious bottle-neck for too long, and more bridges were badly needed to take the ever-increasing traffic across the river. In 1739 London's second bridge

* Another way in which Londoners obtained their water was from the pumping waterwheels below the northern arches of London Bridge, and since early times they had drawn their water from the streams which ran to the river and from springs, wells and conduit heads. Wealthy people had water piped to their houses, but in the streets anyone could buy a jug of water from the cobs—carriers who belonged to the Brotherhood of St Christopher of the Water-bearers. In 1609 Sir Hugh Myddleton, a banker, began the construction of the New River, which, when completed, came winding from the north for forty miles; although it has been made straighter and shorter, it still supplies London with some of its water today. In 1903 all the water supplies were merged into the Metropolitan Water Board, and today most of London's water comes from reservoirs along the Thames banks, well up-river to the west, although some buildings in the city are still served by water from private artesian wells. In the old days, water pipes were made of hollowed tree-trunks, and the joints between them were so poor that at least a quarter of the water leaked away. The first iron water-pipe was used by the Chelsea company in 1746, but wooden pipes were still used until the end of the century.

The first Westminster Bridge, opened in 1751, from a contemporary watercolour. In the background is the Great Hall and the Abbey.

was begun at Westminster, and it was finished twelve years later in 1751. Its designer was a Swiss engineer called Charles Labelye, who produced a graceful stone bridge with fifteen round arches. Sadly enough, it had to be pulled down in 1861, and an ugly iron structure was built in its place.

London's third bridge was begun in 1760 at Blackfriars, by the mouth of the Fleet River, its designer being the architect Robert Mylne. It was first named Pitt Bridge in honour of the Earl of Chatham, who had, according to the foundation tablet of the bridge, 'recovered, augmented and secured the British Empire in Asia, Africa and America, and restored the ancient reputation and influence of his country among the nations of Europe'. This was a fine bridge too, with its nine flattened stone arches, but in 1863 it also was pulled down and replaced by the clumsy structure which is still there today.

A fourth bridge was built at Battersea in 1771, but this was only a rough one of timber. It stood until 1890, and has been recorded in a number of drawings and paintings, notably in the well-known painting at night by Whistler, which hangs in the Tate Gallery.

Old London Bridge was much changed. By 1710 all the houses on it had been rebuilt in the new style, with hipped roofs and deep eaves. In order to widen the roadway to twenty feet, the houses now projected farther over the river. They were in regular terraces, and the old, attractive muddle had gone. Some houses were rebuilt again in 1745 with a colonnade along the road, but by then most of the other houses were in a poor condition, and the Bridge was no longer a fashionable place on which to live.

In 1757 all the houses were pulled down, and London lost its most fascinating and famous sight. The Bridge was widened and partly rebuilt with a wide central arch. Hooded stone alcoves, like those on the new Westminster Bridge, were built above each pier at road level, wherein people could sit in the sunshine and watch the horses and carriages pass. In that state the Bridge stood for another sixty years, although the scour of the river continually washed away parts of the foundations of the Great Arch. Loads of stones were tipped into the water from time to time to try to stop this, but it was a losing battle, and, after New London Bridge was opened in 1831, the old Bridge was at last slowly and sadly demolished.

Some general improvements in and around the City came in the 1760s, such as the laying of raised pavements for pedestrians, the making of sewers and better water supplies, and the lighting of the streets with oil lamps. At the same time many ruinous old buildings and slums, which had existed since Tudor times, were pulled down, together with most of what remained of the old City wall and its gateways.

Two large building projects came to the Strand. One still stands complete; the other has only a few parts left, and they too may soon vanish. The first is the huge, stone building of Somerset House, which, with its several courtyards, covers the site of one of the famous old Strand mansions. Begun in 1776, but not completely finished until 1856, it was built as a public centre to house a number of administrative and academic bodies, such as the tax

New Somerset House was originally built right on the water's edge. Today the Embankment cuts it off from the river.

collectors, the Royal Academy and the Royal Society. These bodies had been scattered in poor premises, but now they had a single, large and monumental home.

Somerset House was an early office block, meant to serve as an impressive symbol for a country which had gained a vast empire. The architect, Sir William Chambers, Surveyor General, Treasurer of the Royal Academy and friend of the King, was a good, but not a great, architect, and his design for Somerset House, though dignified, is dull. Its best feature is the wide terrace and the arcade below it which face the river. When it was built the river lapped right up to the arcade, so that the terrace made a pleasant place on which to stroll and admire the river scene.*

The other project, begun in 1772, and of which only a few parts remain today, was the Adelphi housing scheme. It stood facing the river less than a quarter of a mile to the west of Somerset House, and just east of the York Buildings Waterworks. The architects were Robert Adam and his brother James, and the project was their own business venture; hence the name Adelphi, the Greek word for brothers. The scheme consisted of straight streets of terrace houses, and along the river front was a promenade set above an arcade, like that of Somerset House.

Just as the Whitehall Banqueting Hall had seemed in its time, so did the Adelphi now seem strange and novel to Londoners when it was finished. The walls of yellow brick were decorated with delicate pilasters and plaster ornaments, not unlike those the Ancient Romans had used on their houses long ago. 'Why should our houses look like Roman temples?' asked Robert Adam. 'After all, the Romans themselves did not decorate their homes like temples, but in the way we have done at the Adelphi.'

A very different kind of building was erected on the other side of the river. This was the Albion Mills, completed in 1788 at Bankside, and built four-square and six storeys high, with a tunnel

* The building stands just to the east of Waterloo Bridge. Now, unfortunately, the Victoria Embankment runs in front of Somerset House and cuts it off from the river.

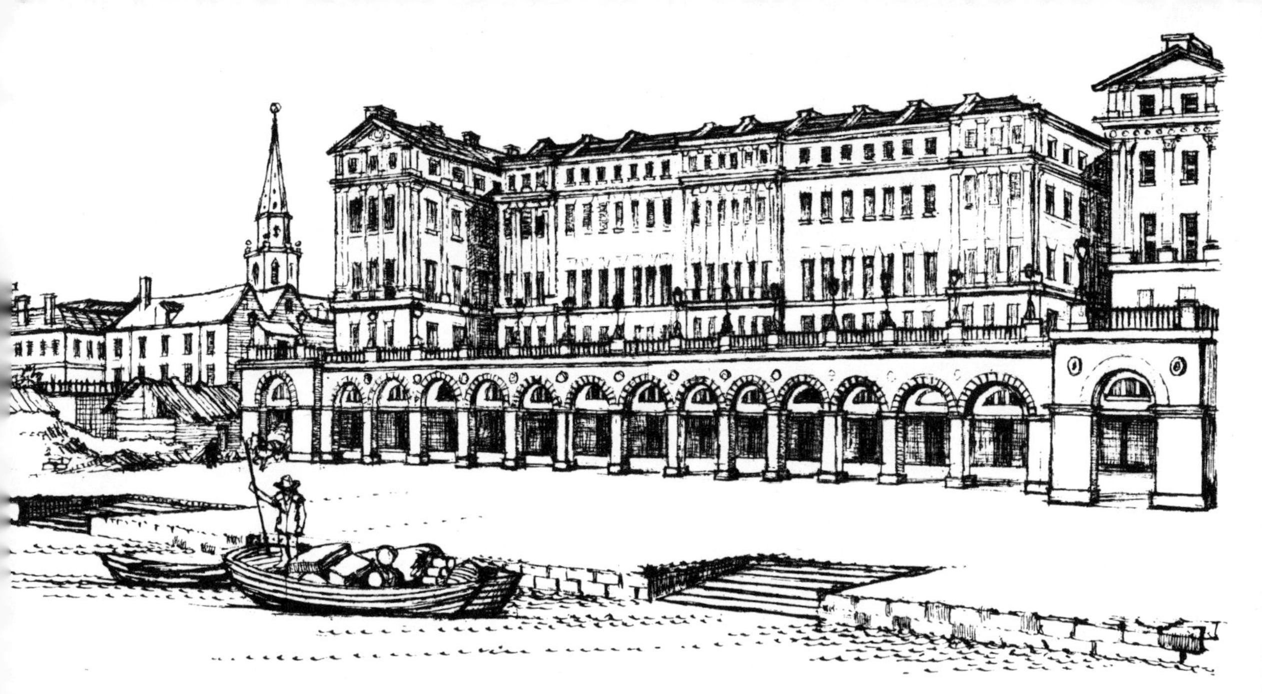

The Adelphi housing scheme, from a print made soon after it was built.

running below it from the river where corn barges could enter. It was a symbol of the age of machines which was beginning in England, because the new steam engines of Boulton and Watt were installed there to drive twenty pairs of mill-stones for grinding corn. The mills were the wonder of their day; they worked well and made high profits. But, only three years after they had been completed, they were destroyed by fire.

On the whole, in spite of its slums, eighteenth-century London was a pleasant place, and, especially after the improvements of the 1760s, it impressed foreign visitors. It could look beautiful from the riverside, when the sun was shining on the dome of St Paul's and on all the white spires of Wren's City churches—as we can see from the drawings, prints, and paintings which artists made at that time, especially those by the Italian painter Canaletto, who visited London.

Not least among the attractions of the town were two pleasure gardens by the river, where people of every sort could enjoy their leisure hours. They were Vauxhall and Ranelagh.

Vauxhall Gardens lay near the south bank of the river above Westminster Bridge, and, although the area has since been built

The City rebuilt after the Fire, from a painting by Canaletto, who visited London during the middle years of the eighteenth century.

over, the name has stayed in the district. The place was already a public resort in the seventeenth century, when it was known as the Spring Gardens of Fawkes Hall. In 1728 a man called Jonathan Tyers took over the lease, and began to improve the place. He opened it four years later with a great banquet attended by Frederick, Prince of Wales, the father of George III, and that was the start of a very successful business, which continued for 130 years—until well into the reign of Queen Victoria.

Nearly every Londoner of the eighteenth century visited the gardens during his life. They were filled with groves of trees hung with tens of thousands of lamps, which were made to light up all together as the evening darkened. In the centre was an orchestra-

The skyline is dominated by the dome of St Paul's Cathedral and the spires of many of Wren's new parish churches.

stand with an organ, surrounded by straight and curving colonnades of booths, or supper-boxes, for dining and wining. These had landscapes and other paintings on their walls—perhaps a scene of a cricket match, or a dance round a maypole.*

A round, gaily decorated building called the Umbrella stood near the centre, where shows of all kinds were held, and where the orchestra could play on wet evenings. There was a Picture Room, and many other structures, including a Chinese Temple, a Hermit's Cottage and a Smugglers' Cave. There was a dimly-lit

* An example of these paintings, called 'The See-saw' by Francis Hayman, can be seen at the Tate Gallery. It shows that the paintings were not merely crude, temporary decorations, but carefully executed works of art.

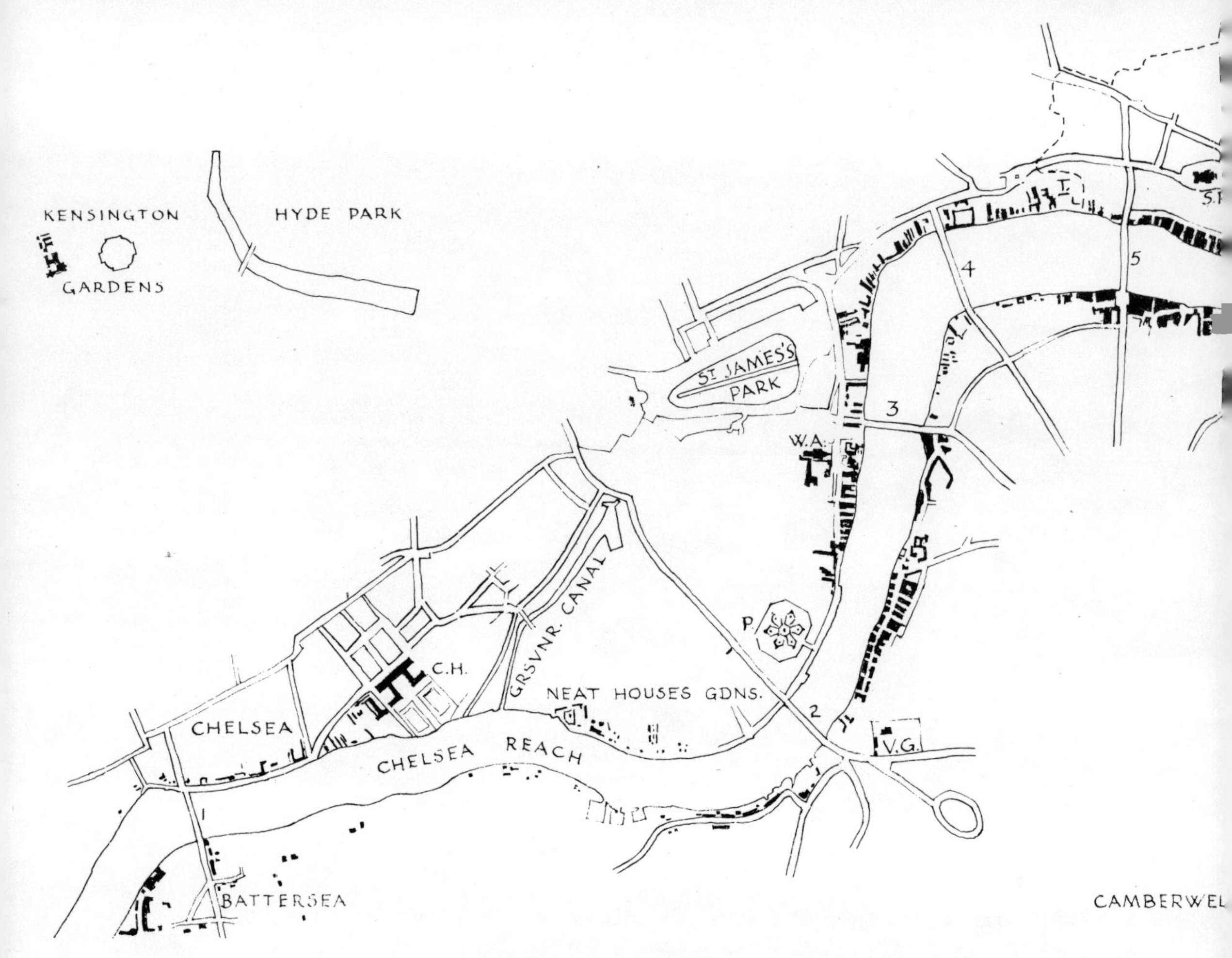

A map of London's riverside in 1827 by Howard Mogg.

BRIDGES: *1. Battersea; 2. Vauxhall; 3. Westminster; 4. Waterloo; 5. Blackfriars; 6. Southwark; 7. London.*

Lovers' Walk, a Cascade which turned a water-mill, and some Musical Bushes, where an orchestra hidden under the ground played fairy music, until the players complained that the dampness ruined their instruments. On special days there were tempests of fireworks, balloon ascents and entertainments by rope-walkers, jugglers and equestrians.

The celebrated Dr Johnson, who sometimes visited the gardens, thought that they were 'peculiarly adapted to the taste of the English nation, there being a mixture of curious show, gay ex-

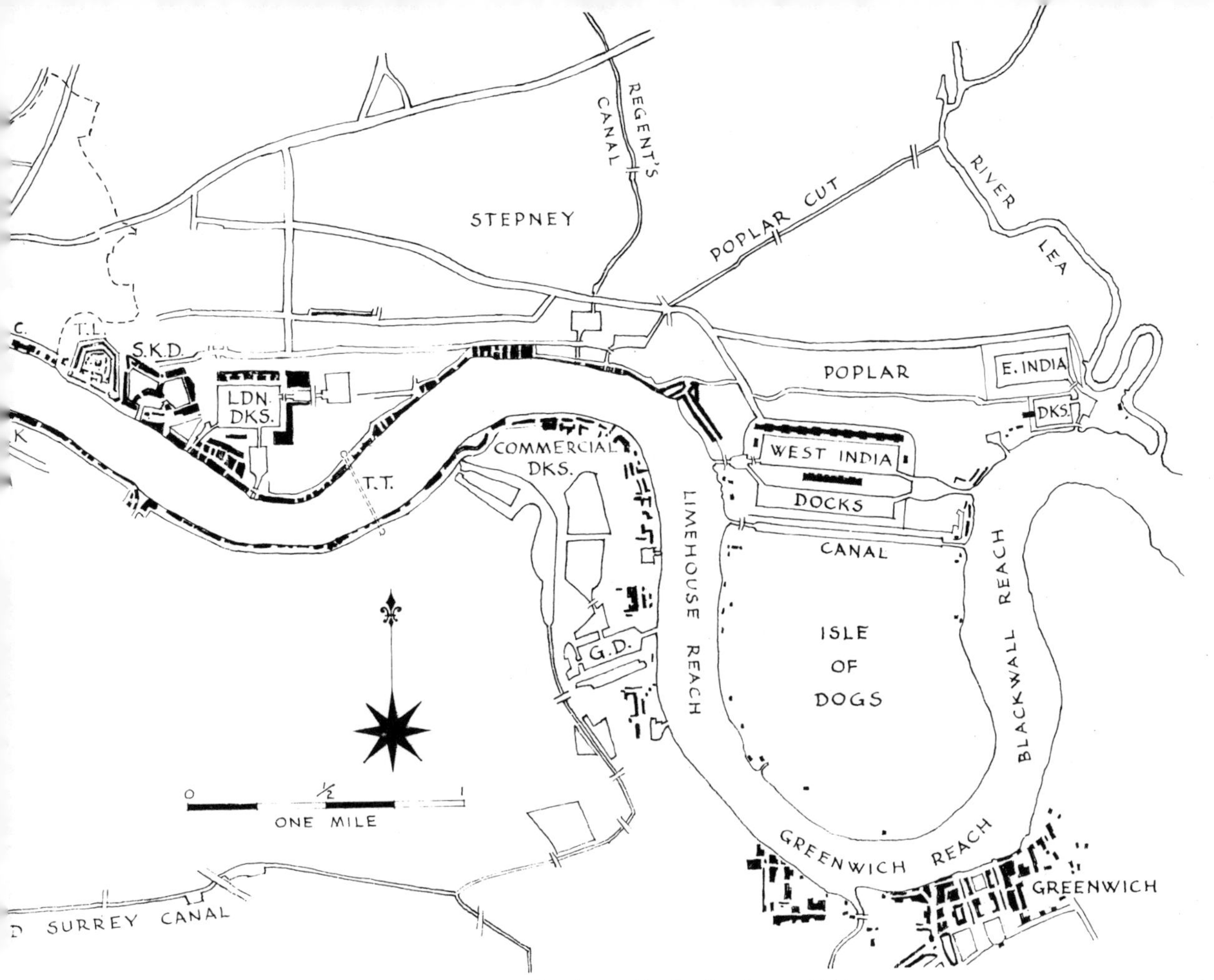

BUILDINGS *etc: C.H. Chelsea Hospital; P. Penitentiary; V.G. Vauxhall Gardens; W.A. Westminster Abbey; T. Temple; S.P. St Paul's Cathedral; M. Monument; C. Customs House; T.L. Tower of London; S.K.D. St Katherine's Docks; T.T. Thames Tunnel; G.D. Greenland Docks.*

hibition, music vocal and instrumental not too refined for the general ear, for all which a shilling is paid'.

Ranelagh was more sedate and fashionable than Vauxhall. It lay on the north bank near the Royal Hospital.* The garden here was less important than a large, round building erected in 1741 and called the Rotunda. This measured 150 feet across, and at its centre rose a gigantic four-sided fireplace, while round the walls

* It was on the spot where the Chelsea Flower Show is held every year now.

Ranelagh by the river at Chelsea, with its grand wooden Rotunda and an ornamental pavilion floating on a decorative 'canal'.

on two floors ran rows of boxes, where parties could eat bread and butter, drink tea, coffee, beer or wine, and watch the famous folk strolling round and round in the light from thousands of candles set in glittering chandeliers.

The Rotunda was all of wood, so it is surprising that, with so many candles burning, it never caught fire during its sixty years of life. Orchestras often played in this fine hall, and there famous musicians gave concerts. Among them was a child prodigy of eight years, who, on a June day in 1764, played pieces of his own composition on the harpsichord and the organ for the benefit of charity. His name was Wolfgang Amadeus Mozart.

Sometimes banquets and fancy-dress balls were held at the Rotunda, but mostly it was used as a promenade. Horace Walpole, the man of fashion and a great letter-writer, often went there. In one of his letters to a friend, he declared that the floor of the Rotunda was 'all of beaten princes'. He added: 'You can't set your foot without treading on a Prince of Wales or Duke of Cumberland. The company is universal; there is from his Grace of Grafton down to children out of the Foundling Hospital—from my Lady Townshend to the kitten.'

On July 8th, 1803—two years before Nelson's victory and death at Trafalgar—the Rotunda opened its doors for the last time. The eighteenth century was over. Yet thirty years were still to pass before the Georgian era, whose most light-hearted and charming aspect was expressed by Vauxhall and Ranelagh, finally came to an end.

C. H. Simpson, Master of Ceremonies at Vauxhall Gardens for thirty-six years. Redrawn from an old lithograph.

CHAPTER VIII

Victorian Steam and Sewers

THE ever-growing momentum of the Industrial Revolution brought overwhelming changes to the whole country in the nineteenth century. Agriculture steadily declined as the basis of English life, and country people flocked to the expanding, industrial towns in search of work. The population of greater London had risen by 1820 to 1,274,000. Then it grew so rapidly that by 1851 it was 2,400,000, and a century later it was over eight millions. In the country as a whole during the same period, the population exploded from about nine-and-a-half millions to over forty millions. So the population was nearly as high in greater London at the end of the century as the whole population of the country had been at its start.

The nineteenth century can be divided for better understanding into two periods, which were clearly reflected in the scenes of the capital and its riverside: the late Georgian and the Victorian. The first lasted until the Great Reform Act of 1832, which gave the vote to the property-owning middle classes, and, until then, England was still an aristocratic country. Beautiful things were still being made by hand, architecture was unified by the classical tradition, and even the new engineering structures, like bridges, canal aqueducts, docks and warehouses, were of simple, noble design. In the West End of Regency London, the architect John Nash brought great changes with his monumental lay-out, reaching from the Mall in the south, through Regent Street, to Regent's Park in the north.

Then, as industries, especially in coal and iron, expanded, and the uncultured middle classes joined in government with the landed gentry, taste rapidly declined. The struggle for money, rather than the cultured life of leisure, became the prime purpose of

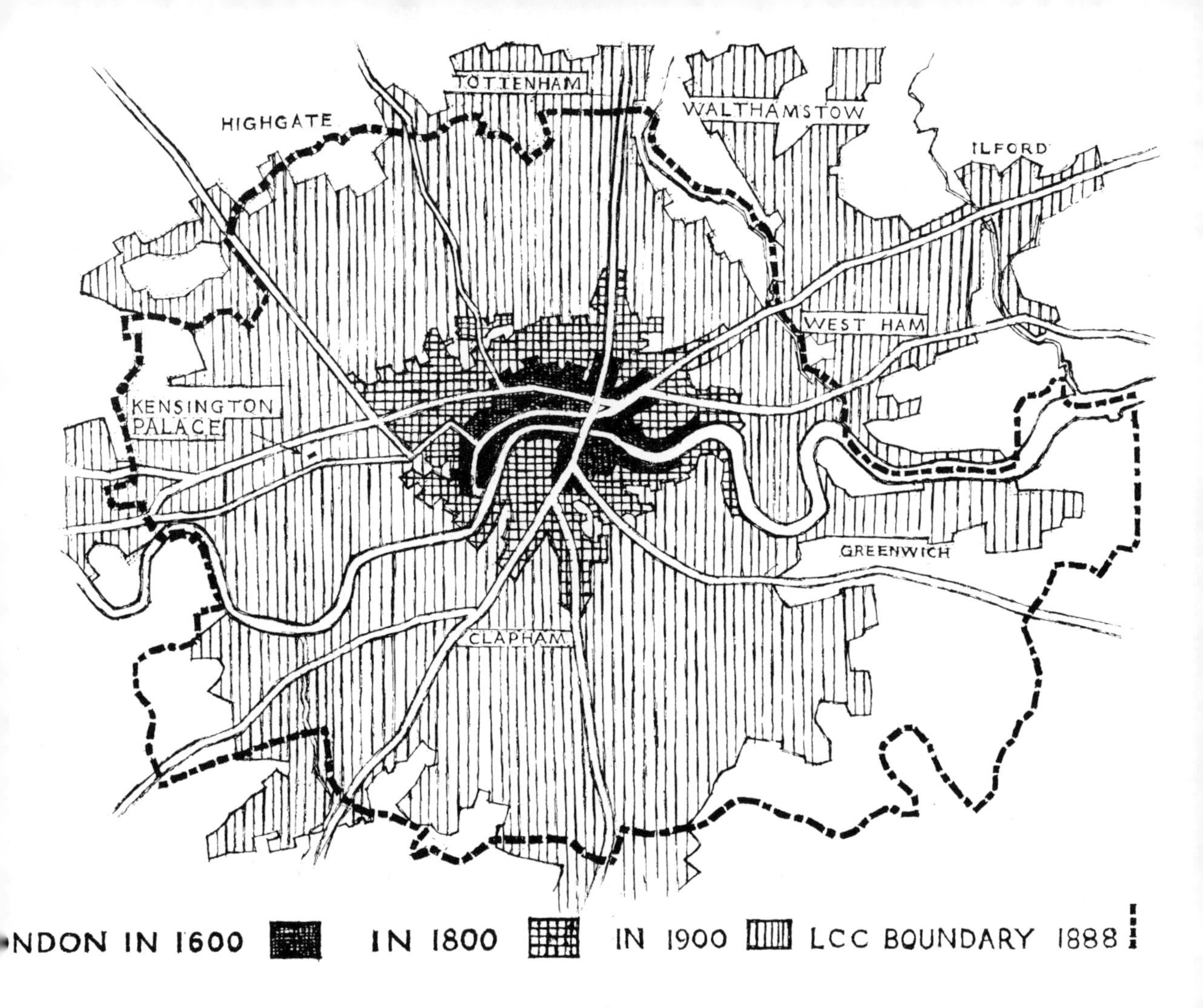

existence. Towns lost their human scale, and grew to huge size in endless mazes of mean, insanitary streets without planning or control. Materials and decorations, mass-made by machines, replaced hand-made production of quality, while architecture became a muddle of styles borrowed from every past age.

But in spite of the unemployment which followed the end of the wars with France, the first three decades of the century were proud years. Napoleon had been defeated, Great Britain now owned a world-wide Empire, and uncontrolled industrialism had not yet spread its full blight over the land.

London was the Imperial City, not only the greatest centre of trade in the world, but now the world centre also of finance. The river was congested with shipping and, even at the century's start, the East India Company alone was sailing more ships from the port than all the vessels of every kind which had sailed there a century before. The situation on the river was becoming impossible.

Ships were still moored densely in mid-stream, and their cargoes were unloaded there into open lighters, which were then moved to the legal quays. The lighters could be unloaded only when the tide was high, and too few warehouses existed where the goods could be stored. Conditions were so bad that a ship might take two months after arriving before it could sail away again. Hogsheads of sugar, barrels of wine and rum, stacks of timber, and all the other cargoes would stand in confused piles in the open for weeks on end, with no one to guard them from thieves, and with no protection from the weather. Pilfering was so common that, at the beginning of the century, the yearly loss from the quays was £500,000, a sum which could buy far more then than it can today.

A river police force was organised, and this, together with heavy penalties, helped to reduce theft, but not to stop it.* The solution came in the form of new, enclosed, and protected docks, surrounded by quays and warehouses, which were dug out of the river banks below the Tower.

These docks were joined to the river by short canals containing locks, in which ships could be raised or lowered as they entered or left the tidal water. In this way, ships could lie quietly in the docks beside the quays in deep water, unaffected by the tides. The goods could be unloaded straight out of the holds with cranes, and then be stored at once in the warehouses. No one who was not entitled

* The Thames Police Force was created in 1798 by Patrick Colquhoun, a magistrate, at the request of the West India merchants, who could no longer bear their losses by theft. In 1829 the Metropolitan Police Force was created by Sir Robert Peel when he was Home Secretary, with 1,000 picked men, who were dressed in a uniform of blue tail-coats, white trousers and top hats, and were armed with truncheons. They were at once nicknamed Peelers or Bobbies after their founder. They replaced the red-waistcoated Bow Street Runners, a body which had been formed in London in the middle of the eighteenth century, and which could no longer deal with mounting crime and rioting. The River Police kept their independence until 1839, when they were joined to the Metropolitan force.

to do so could enter or leave the docks, because the entrances to the streets were few and could be easily guarded.

The first of these docks was opened in 1802 for the West India Company. It lay on the north of the Isle of Dogs, and it had entrances for ships from the river at both ends to a pair of long basins, one for imports, the other for exports. High brick walls and sturdy warehouses five storeys high surrounded the whole. The system worked well, and a number of other docks like it were soon built. Some of these can still be seen in their original form, for instance St Katherine's Docks, opened in 1828, near the Tower at Wapping, which were constructed by the famous early engineer, Thomas Telford. They are fine works, with three basins surrounded by high walls of yellow brickwork.

The new docks were run by private companies, and for a time they made big profits. But as the railways developed and landed goods were moved from the riverside more rapidly, warehouse charges were forced down, and so were the wages of the underpaid dockers. Competition between the companies grew fierce, and strikes by dock workers became increasingly frequent. These troubles were to produce another crisis in the docks at the end of the century.

Days of sail at St Katherine's Docks, Wapping.

The ships with their tall masts and square, white sails, which came sailing up river to moor in the new docks, grew larger and slimmer, until, when the half-century had passed, they reached their final perfection in the beautiful clippers, or wind-jammers, which carried tea from India and China, and wool and grain from Australia.

To sail these ships required much skill, and their captains and crews took great pride in their craft. They would race each other home across the oceans with superb performance, straining every mast, spar and rope with as many sails as they dared to unfurl—and often more.*

As the century advanced, more and more ships were powered by steam engines using coal as fuel, and more and more were made of iron instead of wood. To begin with, the engines turned great paddle wheels fixed at the sides of the ships, and the ships had sails as well as engines if they were large enough to go to sea. Later on screw propellers replaced paddle wheels.

The first steam-ship was seen on the river in 1801. After 1815 steam and packet-boats, with their tall, thin funnels and frothing paddle wheels, were a daily sight, and from 1840 onwards for several decades, local passenger steam-boats plied up and down the river. These Penny Steamers, as they were called, continued the work of the watermen who had been carrying Londoners about the river in their small boats for centuries. But in time travel on the river seemed slow compared with the new horse-buses, trams and trains which ran on land, and so most of the waterbuses eventually disappeared.† The river above the docks became ever more dull and lifeless, as fewer and fewer boats enlivened it.

But the docks down river were—and, indeed, still are—lively

* One of these clippers, with its carved figurehead of a woman still urging her ship forward below the long bowsprit, has been preserved in a special dry dock by the riverside at Greenwich, and can be visited. She is the famous *Cutty Sark*, launched as late as 1869.

† River steamers have returned to some extent now, and several companies run sightseeing tours on the river which stop at various landing stages as far down as Greenwich and as far up as Hampton Court.

A nineteenth-century clipper.

enough. In thc 1870s, before all the sailing ships had vanished, the writer Richard Jefferies was able to describe the fascinating dockland he knew:

'It is a great plain: a plain of enclosed waters, built in and restrained by the labour of man, and holding upon its surface fleet upon fleet, argosy upon argosy. Masts to the right, masts to the left, masts in front, masts yonder above the warehouses; masts across the river hung with drooping half-furled sails; masts afar down thin and attenuated, mere dark straight lines in the distance. They await in stillness the rising of the tide.'

By the century's close, hardly a single mast for sail could be seen towering above the walls and warehouses of the docks, to set one dreaming of adventurous voyages to far-off, unknown lands. The romantic, age-old days of sail were over.

Up river from the new docks, London Bridge was built anew in 1831, to a simple design in stone by the Scottish engineer John Rennie. Then the old Bridge, a hundred feet to its east, which had served London so well for so long, was demolished. Now seven road bridges crossed the river—Battersea, Vauxhall, Westminster, Waterloo, Blackfriars, Southwark and London. A century later, there stood between Battersea in the west down to Tower Bridge* in the east, no less than eleven road bridges and four railway bridges.

Another crossing—running not over but under the river—was begun in 1825. This was the Thames Tunnel, the first of its kind. Dug through the bed of the river, it linked the dock district of Wapping on the north bank with Rotherhithe on the south. Its purpose was to take wheeled traffic, but the spiral ramps at either

* Tower Bridge, opened in 1894, is London's most interesting bridge. Standing just below the Tower, it is the last Thames bridge before the sea. With its heavy, towering piers, in some curious sort of Flemish mediaeval style, it forms a monumental gateway to London's river. It is the only movable bridge on the Thames. The roadway is made to lift upwards in two leaves by hydraulic power, so that quite large ships can pass through into the Pool. For its period, it was a considerable engineering feat, and to this day it works hard and well.

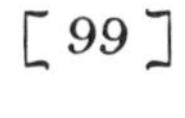

The 'Comet', an early steam boat.

Building New London Bridge, from an engraving made in 1833 by Edward Cooke. On the left the old Bridge still stands, with its central arch greatly widened and its houses gone.

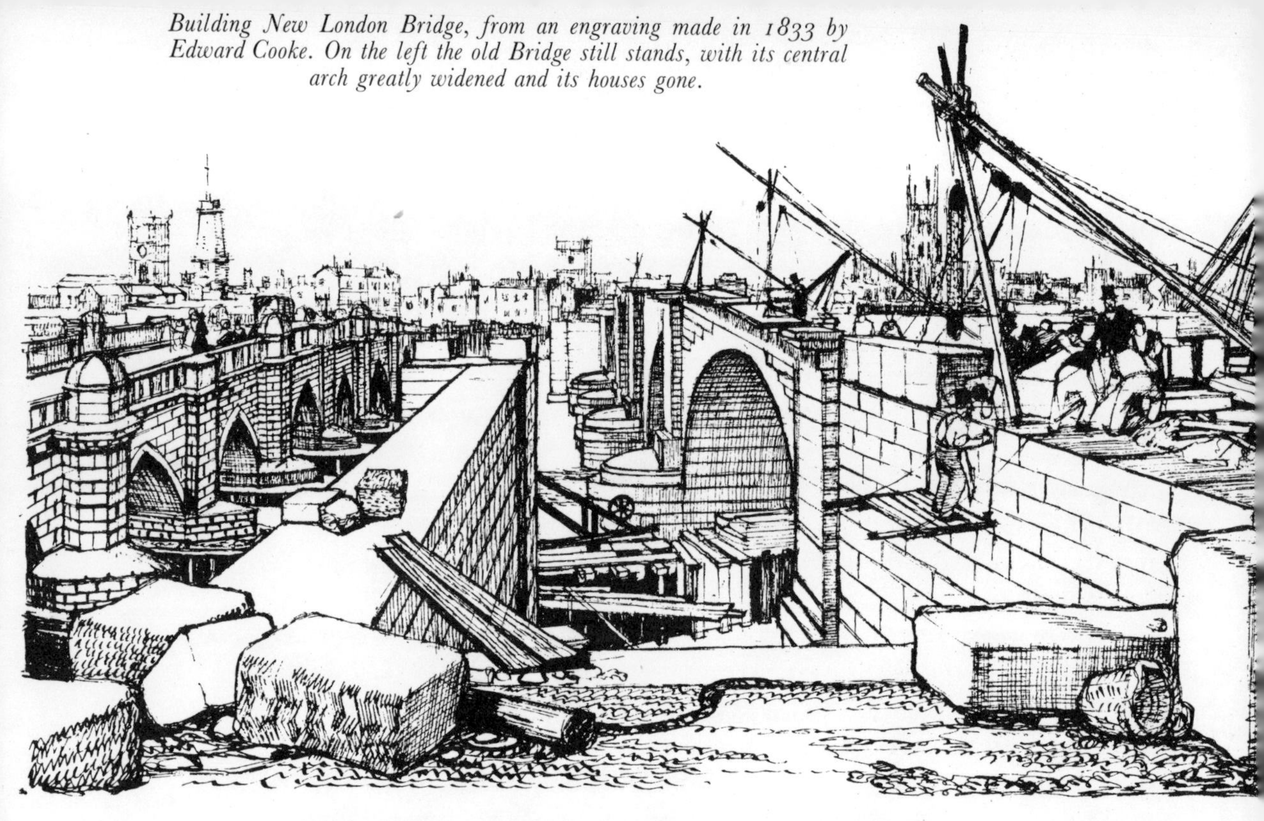

end, down which carts and carriages could have reached the tunnel, were never built, and, for some time after it was finished, only foot-passengers could use it. In that sense it was a failure, but it now serves as a useful railway tunnel.

Although the tunnel was not a financial success, it was one of those heroic feats of early, experimental engineering for which Britain had become famous. The engineer was Marc Isambard Brunel, a Frenchman by birth who had settled in England, and he was helped by his young son, Isambard Kingdom Brunel, who later became a great railway and bridge builder.*

* Though his main work was on the Great Western Railway, the younger Brunel had another link with London's river, apart from the Tunnel. He designed the huge, fabulous steamship, *The Great Eastern*, which was built and launched at Millwall in 1858. Because the river was narrow here, she was launched sideways. Seven hundred feet long, and powered by paddle wheels and a propeller, she was designed to travel to Australia and back, carrying her own coal all the way. After this, Thames-side ship-building gradually died, partly because the river was too narrow for launching the large, new ships of iron (and later steel), which were being built, and partly because London was not well situated for the supply of iron.

First a shaft was dug at Rotherhithe, and the twin arches of the tunnel were begun. The digging was done with the help of a moving shield of twelve cast-iron frames, supporting a wall of wooden boards. This shield was moved forward in short stages by turning some huge screws. Each frame was divided into three compartments, one above the other, and in each compartment stood two workmen. The man in front removed some of the wooden boards, and dug away the earth behind them to a depth of nine inches (a brick's length), and then he replaced the boards in their new position. The man behind him laid a few bricks of the tunnel arch. Then the frame was moved forward nine inches by turning the big screws at the back of the frame. The twelve frames were not all moved forward at the same time, but alternately. When the work was going well, about eight feet of tunnel could be built in a week.

But the work did not always go well. Many stoppages were caused when mud and water poured in. Then the river itself broke into the tunnel when the side of an unknown pit, which had been dredged at some time in the river bed, was pierced. The whole tunnel was flooded. Two months later came another, and very sudden, flood. Young Brunel was in the tunnel at the time, but by good luck he was carried by the force of the water to the top of the shaft. Others were not so lucky, and six men were drowned.

By the end of August 1836, the middle of the river had been passed. More troubles followed, for the water burst in three more times. Sometimes sewer gas from the dirty river entered the tunnel, together with black, half-fluid mud. The gas often exploded, and flashes of fire would pass twenty-five feet across the shield. The work was therefore not only dangerous but unhealthy, and men would sometimes fall senseless in their frames, or be suddenly struck blind by Tunnel Sickness.

The bitter struggle went doggedly on. At last the north bank was reached, and the shaft was sunk to meet it. On March 25th, 1843, the tunnel was opened to the public with a great ceremony, when the little, old engineer, Sir Marc, who had been knighted for his work, marched at the head of a procession through the Great

Bore, as it was now called, behind a band of fifes and drums. Over eighteen years had been spent in 'putting a pipe into old Thames's mouth'.

About a mile to the east of Westminster on the north bank, another undertaking had been completed in 1821, four years before the Thames Tunnel had been started. This was the huge prison called the Penitentiary, which was built in a star shape with the Governor's house at the centre, and contained a thousand cells linked by three miles of corridors. The notorious 'Tench' was dreaded by criminals, for it was not only damp and gloomy, but there back-breaking, futile labour was forced on the prisoners, such as moving cannon-balls or sand from one pile to another hour after hour and day after day, or walking for hours on an endless treadmill. Those who were marched out of this riverside hell into boats on the river, and thence down the Thames to ships which

The entrance to the Thames Tunnel, from an engraving in 'The Illustrated London News'. The Tunnel was begun in 1825, but not opened until 1843.

would sail them to the penal settlements of Australia, must have been happy men.

Although everyone disliked this gloomy castle, it remained until 1890. Then more humane buildings took its place: an early housing estate built by the London County Council, and the world-famous Tate Gallery of Art, completed in 1897, which was presented to the nation by Sir Henry Tate, the sugar millionaire.

During the first half of the century, prisons, even more horrible than the Tench, existed on the river itself, in the form of worn-out hulks of naval ships. Here also, for a time, prisoners were detained in appalling conditions while awaiting transportation, and many were employed during the day on building the new, enclosed docks.

In the London of the earlier, Georgian, part of the nineteenth century, the fine old mediaeval Great Hall, with its masterly timber roof, St Stephen's Chapel right on the riverside, and the nearby Abbey gave some dignity to Westminster, but between and around them stood a mean, unplanned jumble of buildings of all shapes, sizes, ages and conditions which served as government offices. The area was not a fit symbol for the Law* and Government of a powerful nation which ruled a great empire, and the undignified mess surprised and shocked foreign visitors.

Then one autumn evening in 1834, bundles of old tally-sticks for counting money were pushed into a stove below the House of Lords. In the intense heat some wooden panels nearby caught fire, and soon all the government buildings that made up the 'Palace of Westminster' were blazing. Many of them had wooden frames covered with laths and plaster, and so the fire travelled fast.

Excited crowds, held back by three regiments of Guards, watched the flames spread. They gathered in boats on the river, or stood knee-deep in the river water; they thronged on to Westminster Bridge, and filled the streets all around. Each time a flame burst into the darkening sky, the crowds greeted it with a great cheer, which added to the din of the roaring, crackling blaze.

* The Law Courts had been fixed at Westminster since 1225, and at this time seven Courts clustered to the west of the Great Hall. They were moved to new buildings in the Strand just north of the Temple in 1882.

The burning of the old Houses of Parliament in 1834. In the centre is St Stephen's Chapel, which had long been used as the Debating Chamber of the House of Commons.

Not until three o'clock in the morning was the fire at last under control. Happily the Great Hall had been saved, but little else remained, and St Stephen's Chapel was a ruin. However, the show had been a fine one, and regrets were few.

What should be done to re-house Parliament? Many ideas were offered. William IV said he would allow Buckingham Palace to be used, and the Green Park near the Palace was suggested as a site. Yet no one really wanted Parliament to leave its historic position by the river. In any case, as the Duke of Wellington pointed out, the Houses of Parliament should be built where they could never be completely surrounded by a mob, and the river would prevent this at Westminster.

So the old site was chosen for the new Parliament buildings, and an architectural competition was held. It was won by Charles Barry, and it is his design in the revived Gothic style that we see today, with its towers, pinnacles and intricately carved walls—including the famous clock tower which holds the great, cracked bell called Big Ben.

In the romantic style of its period, it was very well designed, especially in the lay-out of its various parts and rooms. Its carved details were good too, both inside and out, and these were designed not by the architect, but by Augustus Pugin, an inspired artist who unfortunately went mad and died at an early age. The stone of the buildings was badly chosen, however, for the smoky air of London has been turning it slowly into Epsom Salts ever since.

Although the new Houses of Parliament were begun in 1837, the complex whole was not fully completed until 1860. These years covered early Victorian times, and saw a period of uncontrolled expansion of towns and industries. The new railways were taking over most of the country's transport, both of goods and passengers, from the coaching roads and from the network of canals which now covered the country. Already by 1843 two thousand miles of railway had been built in Great Britain, and by the end of the five years of Railway Mania which followed, no less than five thousand miles had been built.

The new Iron Horses altered the scene on London's river, for on its banks great terminal railway stations arose at Charing Cross, Cannon Street and London Bridge, with sweeping arches of iron and glass so magnificent that such structures have been called the Cathedrals of Victorian England. A number of new railway bridges were also built to cross the river, but none of these was either impressive or beautiful.

Although the Municipal Reform Act of 1835 gave the vote to ratepayers in local elections, only by slow stages did local governments become aware of their responsibilities. Social improvements came very gradually in London in the form of better street lighting,

A Victorian horse bus.

Cannon Street Station, a typical Victorian railway terminus with a soaring roof of iron and glass, from a print of 1866. The view is from the railway bridge which crosses the river. Most of the building has now been pulled down.

better sanitation, roads and transport, new schools, hospitals, public baths, libraries and museums, and the preservation of open spaces for public parks and gardens. Slowly town governments, in London as elsewhere, also began to supply gas, water and, in time, electricity, and even public transport in the form of trams.*

* Right up to our own times, most public transport was run by private companies, including the Underground Railway system, which developed in London during the later decades of the nineteenth century. In the streets of Victorian London traffic jams of horse-buses, carriages, hansom cabs, drays and saddle horses, were frequent, and to remedy the congestion, the first underground railway, nicknamed the Sewer Railway, was opened in 1863 between Paddington and Farringdon Street. At first, the carriages were open trucks, pulled by steam engines. In 1890 the first electric tube line, the South London Tube which runs from the City to Stockwell, was opened and since then the tube system of the London Transport Executive has been spreading its tentacles ever farther out into the twentieth-century suburbs.

In spite of the dull ugliness of its buildings, so-called Gas-and-Water Socialism was a blessing. Without it, terrible epidemics might have occurred, and also serious social disturbances. Slumdom and poverty went on all the same in the growing industrial towns and in London's East End, right through the century and beyond. Amidst the beauty and romance of the shipping, squalor, misery and crime were part of everyday life around the docks. Charles Dickens, among other writers, vividly described them, for he knew them well, and the artist Gustave Doré drew dramatic pictures of dockland for the book called *London*.

By contrast, large, new, comfortable middle-class houses were built in the West End. Between Westminster and Chelsea, a wide, flat, windy space had always existed. There Westminster schoolboys hunted wildfowl on autumn afternoons, and there, right up to the nineteenth century, footpads molested late travellers when nights were black. A large part of this area was built up during the first half of the century as housing estates composed of squares and streets of terrace houses, faced with white stucco, and having the classical porticoes and basement kitchens which are typical of middle-class Victorian London. These were the districts of riverside Pimlico and the more fashionable Belgravia to its north. They were erected by Thomas Cubitt, a speculative builder, who, unlike most of his sort, was a good one. His work represents an interesting architectural link between Georgian and Victorian London and much of it still stands.

Right along the riverside past Pimlico, reaching all the way to the corner of the old City at Blackfriars to the east and to Chelsea in the west, important riverside developments were completed between 1870 and 1874. These were the new Embankments, with their wide roadways, heavy granite walls, and elaborate lamp-posts of cast-iron decorated with dolphins and other devices, which were designed by the engineer Sir Joseph Bazalgette, for the Metropolitan Board of Works.*

* This Board was the forerunner of the London County Council, which was formed in 1889 to co-ordinate the work of many small bodies. In 1965 the L.C.C. was re-organised under the title Greater London Council or G.L.C.

The Embankment to the west was called Chelsea, and that to the east Victoria, while across the river, facing Westminster and Millbank, a similar embankment was built, which was called the Albert. These structures were a great achievement, not only in helping traffic, reclaiming land and controlling floods, but also in containing large, new sewers in the soil below the roadways. Until they were built and the whole drainage system of London was replanned, sewage disposal had been so poor that slum-dwellers often lived on top of cess-pools, which caused serious outbreaks of cholera during the mid-century years.

In 1847 all cess-pools were forbidden, some 100,000 of them were closed, and the sewage of London was then made to flow into the Thames. The river thus became a huge, open sewer. Fish could no longer live in the filthy water, and the stench which arose from it became so horrible that sometimes Members of Parliament at Westminster would agree to stop their debating and go home. In

The Embankment at Chelsea in 1874 soon after its completion, from an engraving in 'Pictorial World'. On the left is Chelsea Old Church, destroyed during the Second World War but now rebuilt as before.

the hot summer of 1858 came the climax, known as the Great Stink. The situation was now so bad that the authorities were forced into the action which led to the building of the Embankments and of the new sewage-disposal scheme with which they were linked. In that system, drains ran down to the large pipes running on both sides of the river, which continued for many miles to the east of London towards special outfalls. There the sewage was treated, and soon it was loaded on to ships and carried out to sea, where it could be dumped. In spite of this and other more recent improvements, London's river, even today, is far from clean.

After mid-century the expansion of the population and building of greater London was explosive and one outlying village after another became absorbed into the capital. Happily, in the ever-spreading wilderness of yellow brickwork and grey-slated roofs, two pleasant green and open public spaces were preserved on the riverside. One was Battersea Park on the south bank opposite Chelsea, which was opened in 1858, thanks mainly to the vision of the builder Cubitt. It was a wild, wet, marshy area, and its whole surface had to be raised. This was done chiefly by unloading on it the excavated earth from the Victoria Dock, east of the Isle of Dogs, which was then under construction, and from there, and from other sources, a million cubic yards of earth were carried along the river in barges to raise up the land for the new park. At first the scene was barren indeed, but soon trees, grass and flowers began to grow, so that today Battersea Park is a refreshingly leafy playground with a boating lake, and, since 1951, a lively fun-fair too.

The other riverside park was Cremorne, which covered twelve acres of ground up-river on the north bank to the west of Chelsea.* Cremorne was not unlike Vauxhall, and for about sixteen years the two pleasure gardens existed together, for Cremorne opened in 1843 and Vauxhall did not close until 1859. Although it had its own charm, Cremorne was not so fashionable as Ranelagh had been, nor even Vauxhall in its hey-day, and it was patronised mostly by cheerful Cockney crowds.

* Where the Lots Road Power Station now stands.

A balloon ascent at Cremorne Gardens in 1859, from a contemporary journal. The gardens occupied the site where Lot's Road power station now stands.

On the river bank stood a great iron gateway, where the Penny Steamers landed their passengers. In the grounds the main feature was a band-stand, surrounded by a wide dance-floor, where the stove-pipe hats and poke bonnets bobbed and turned on summer evenings. There was a Pagoda, a Circus, a Playhouse, a Banqueting Hall, a Marionette Theatre and, among other buildings set between the trees, a Swiss chalet and an Indian temple. Like Vauxhall, Cremorne had its special spectacles, as when Selina Young, the Female Blondin, crossed the Thames here on a tight-rope, or when Madame Poitevin, seated on a heifer, rose to the clouds in a balloon.

As the years passed, Cremorne became increasingly rowdy—finally to a point of scandal. Its owner was now in serious debt, and, at the end of the season of 1877, its gates were closed for ever.

Let us leave Victorian London, not with the din of a dockers' fist-fight for a day's work in the raw fog of dawn down in Wapping, but more pleasantly, with the waves of a waltz floating down river from Cremorne through a soft summer night. In spite of its vast changes and its rigid class differences, life was to remain until the end of the century and for fourteen years beyond, stable enough on the surface. London was the hub of a huge empire and the great city sprawled ever farther from the grimy river over the surrounding marshes. Within its brickwork jungle still lay many attractive Georgian retreats; dignified carriages still clattered through the West End squares, for motor-cars had not yet revolutionised life in the town.

A hansom cab in late Victorian London.

CHAPTER IX

Today and Tomorrow

WHAT of London and its river in this twentieth century of ours? The effects of two world wars, the internal combustion engine and extraordinary technical developments in every field have changed life completely. We live in remarkable times—of instability, anxiety, conflict and ugliness, but also of great hope for the future.

The British Empire has been broken down, and most of the old colonies have become self-governing states within a loosely-knit Commonwealth. Since the coming of the aeroplane, submarine and atom bomb, Britain's island position no longer gives protection and strength.

As we have seen, the situation at the London docks at the end of the nineteenth century was unsatisfactory. Drastic action had to be taken, and in 1909, the Port of London Authority was formed to unite all the interests into a single body, which could take charge of the whole of London's river and its docks. The P.L.A. does its work well, and has so improved the port that the shipping which arrives and departs is many million tons a year, while a million tons of goods can be stored under cover at one time. The docks have continued to expand. In 1921 the King George V Dock was dug, and that made another link in the Royal Dock group, which lies east of the Isle of Dogs at the mouth of the River Lea. Making 246 acres of water in all, this group forms the widest area of impounded dock water in the world. More docks have been built down river too. Lately, however, London has lost much trade because of obsolete methods and equipment among other things. The City docks in particular have become moribund and the whole area is being rebuilt.

Although the river, the port and the old merchant City at the

Shipping in the Pool of London above Tower Bridge today.

core still hold the huge tangled growth of greater London together and still provide its first meaning, London has another meaning now. It has become so vast a market place that it attracts people towards it like a magnet, just because it is so vast.

At the centre, the Square Mile of the ancient mercantile City has kept its old traditions. It has retained its own government, for this has not become absorbed by the Greater London Council, which governs the rest of greater London. A good deal of the City has remained unchanged since Victorian times, and it still holds many interesting relics from the past, in spite of the serious bomb damage of the Second World War. Most of the bombed sites have now been built over with large, and often tower-like, office blocks

Battersea Power Station.

with steel or concrete frames faced with glass. They have been laid out with little co-operation, co-ordination or thought, and, as after the Great Fire, so in our own times after the bombing, too little has been done to rebuild the City in a sensible way.

One wide, bombed area to the north of the City, called the Barbican, however, has been rebuilt as a complete planned district designed as a whole for living in, and dominated by a cluster of towers of flat dwellings. This will be a valuable experiment for future rebuilding in other places, where worn-out parts of old towns are renewed, not in the old, haphazard way, but with well-considered planning of buildings, roads and open spaces, as complete districts in which the inhabitants could enjoy a pleasanter life than they do now.

Many new buildings have appeared along the riverside during this century. Battersea on the south bank of the river, and Chelsea, which faces it on the north bank, with its charming Cheyne Walk of eighteenth-century houses, its Embankment and its two Victorian bridges of Battersea and the Royal Albert, have changed very little. But at Pimlico, a large new housing estate of flats has replaced many of Cubitt's terraces. On the opposite side of the river rises a great building which symbolises our age: the famous Battersea Power Station with its four chimneys pouring out plumes of white smoke. It makes a dramatic picture across the river on a misty night, when ships and cranes form a black pattern low down against the towering, floodlit walls of pink brickwork.

At Millbank, beyond the Tate Gallery, the great office tower of the Vickers Company has altered the skyline. This is better and more honest architecture than the large, clumsy office blocks faced with white stone lying just to its east, which were built between the two world wars. Yet these new towers, which have changed

A modern office building. The Vickers Tower on Millbank.

London's skyline, all look so much alike that we are beginning to find them rather dull because they have been designed without any love or pleasure. The way most of the people inside them spend large parts of their lives is often dull too, though, happily, the work they do may soon become unnecessary as machines begin to accomplish more and more of the daily toiling for us.

Facing the Tate Gallery, on the south bank, a range of new office buildings has appeared, all unrelated to one another and so expressing the commercial competition of our times.

At the south end of Westminster Bridge, a little farther east, lie the headquarters of the Greater London Council, a long, monumental, classical building by the river, which was begun in 1878, but finished, at least along the river front, only in 1922. To its east stands an important new building. It is the Royal Festival Hall, completed for the London County Council in 1951

The main concert hall with its rows of projecting boxes of the Royal Festival Hall during an interval in a concert.

mainly as a permanent concert hall, which formed at the time it was built a part of the temporary 1951 Festival of Britain Exhibition held in this area. The outside is clumsy, but the inside is beautifully designed and is one of the few new additions to the cultural life of the capital of which Londoners can feel proud.

The area around the Festival Hall was to have been developed by the L.C.C. after 1951 as a cultural centre, but, as funds were not forthcoming, an oil company acquired the site. It built a brutal, square tower of offices to the east of the Festival Hall, and so London lost another chance of good local planning.

Just below this Shell Tower, the river is spanned by the new Waterloo Bridge, completed in 1945. It replaced John Rennie's old Waterloo Bridge of stone, which had been opened in 1817 on the second anniversary of the Battle of Waterloo. The new bridge is of reinforced concrete, faced with stone slabs, and it can claim, with its long, low, leaping arches,* to be the finest of all the existing bridges across the Thames. To its west, on the south bank, stands the new Hayward Gallery, a film theatre and concert halls, and across the bridgehead, the National Theatre.

Farther down river, the skyline is broken by new towers and chimneys but Rennie's London Bridge has gone to Arizona and and a new bridge of concrete has taken its place, while beyond it, as the gateway to London's river, Tower Bridge raises its familiar silhouette. This is still the last bridge before the sea, but the Dartford tunnel has now been completed far down river.

Nobody can claim that London today is an inspiring sight. The best is what remains from past centuries, and its moments of beauty occur by accident rather than by design, especially beside the river at night when the lights come on and begin to dance on the water. London has grown with little forethought or planning, and mainly as a result of speculative enterprise. A minority of people has been allowed to build just how and where it likes, with the sole aim of making money, and the result is architectural chaos. Some laws exist to control building and planning, but they are mostly restrictive and uncreative in their effects.

* They are not, in fact, true arches, for this is a beam bridge.

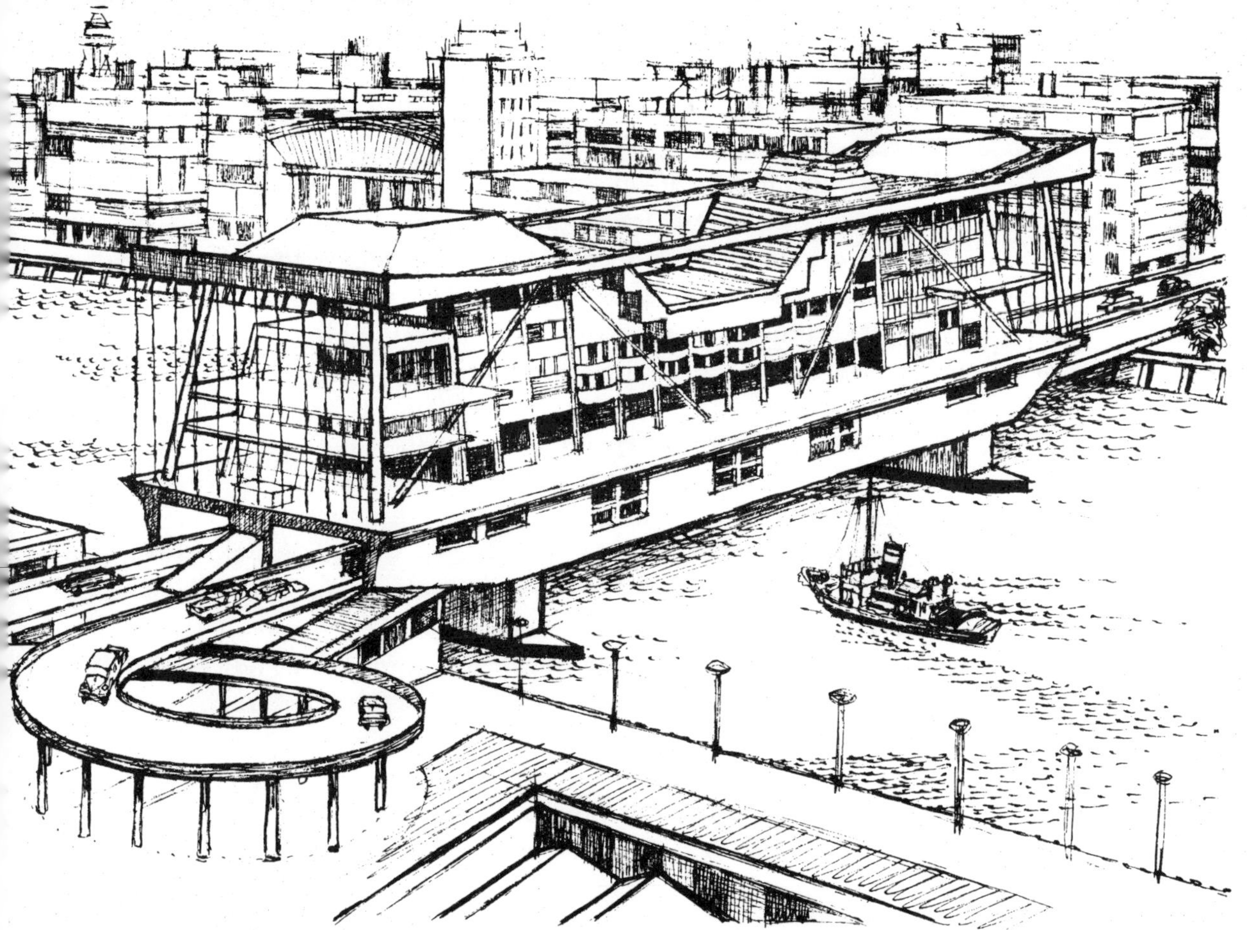

A project for a new bridge having buildings on it like Old London Bridge. Called Crystal Span and designed by a group of well-known architects and engineers for the glass-making firm of Pilkingtons, it would contain an art gallery, an hotel, a theatre, a skating rink and shops.

If London is to become a beautiful city, more creative planning will be needed. In order to make the town and its riverside less seedy, and living and working there much easier, a number of plans were prepared during and after the Second World War.† If they were carried out, the riverside would have more open spaces along it, and give easier access for pedestrians to the banks, so that the Londoner would feel less cut off from his river than he does now. But so far very little has been achieved.

† The important plans are, *The County of London* by Forshaw and Abercrombie of 1943, *The Greater London Region Plan* by Abercrombie of 1944 and *The City of London Plan* by Holden and Holford of 1946. New plans with ring roads have been prepared about which much argument goes on.

In rebuilding our towns we have to know clearly how we want to live in them, and for what purposes. We must realise that, though a town comes into existence for the sake of life—for marketing, and distributing food, for example—it continues to exist for the good life, with all those arts, entertainments, charms and pleasures, which only large communities can provide.

Before we can imagine how London and its riverside could look in the future, we must first imagine what kind of life is possible for its inhabitants. Science and machines now offer a high quality of living for everyone, with far more spare time than has ever been possible before in history. They offer a new freedom—the freedom from poverty and back-breaking toil. With the fear of poverty gone, co-operation for mutual benefit could become easier, so that everyone would want to see their town replanned and rebuilt for pleasure and leisure, and might also want to take part themselves in the creative effort.

London could be a clean and peaceful town, not dirty, noisy and filled with restless people, rushing anxiously to and from their work in crowded trains and buses. The stress need not be only on the enforced daily grind, but on free, cultural, creative and sporting activities of all kinds. Because more time would be available for educating people in how to enjoy life, they would become interested in their neighbourhoods and their whole city—in their fascinating past as well as in how they worked and looked in the present; in the shapes buildings and trees made against the sky; in the views down streets, and the feeling they gave of something worth exploring round the corner; in the way old buildings and new were blended together to make delightful pictures; in colours of materials and paint-work; in the way pavements were laid to make pleasing textures and patterns; in the designs of small objects like street lamps, doors, windows, window boxes and sculpture; in the way changes of level were handled; in the design of open spaces and public gardens and, last but not least, in the planting of trees.

In the new London, traffic could be separated by drastic means from pedestrians, in the way railways are now, and the whole town could be broken down into definite districts, based on the old villages and small towns which have been eaten up in the general, shapeless sprawl. The districts could be separated from one another by wide roads running through wooded parklands, and each would thus tend to develop its own special character.

The river itself might undergo a big change, because an old idea, first proposed in 1858, could at last be carried out. That is the building of a barrage, or dam, across the river below the City, so that the river above the dam could be tideless and flow along with slow dignity always at the same high level, and in one direction, towards the sea.

The dam could be built fairly far down the river, below the docks—probably at Woolwich—and contain locks to allow ships to pass up and down. And it could carry a road to serve as another bridge across the river.

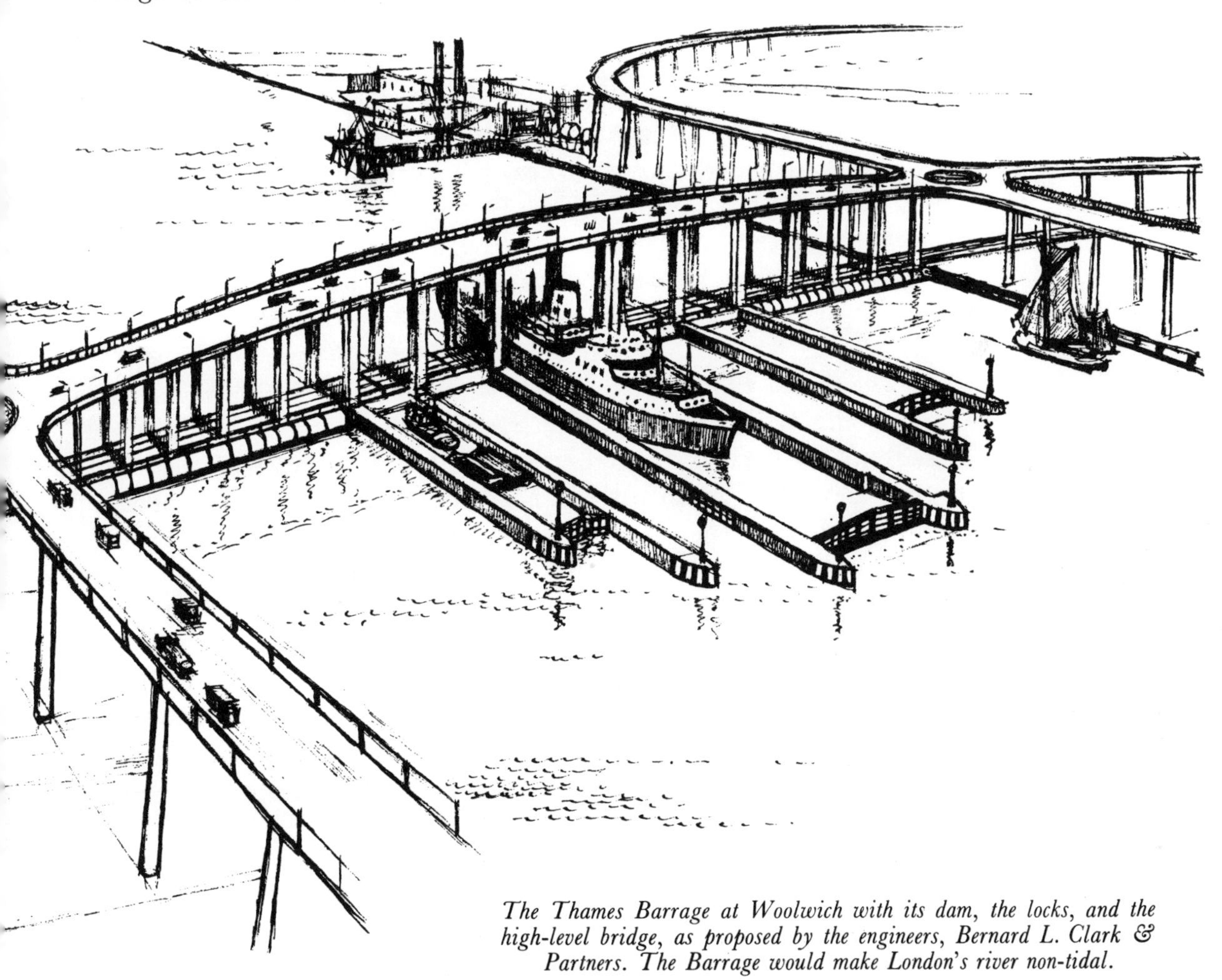

The Thames Barrage at Woolwich with its dam, the locks, and the high-level bridge, as proposed by the engineers, Bernard L. Clark & Partners. The Barrage would make London's river non-tidal.

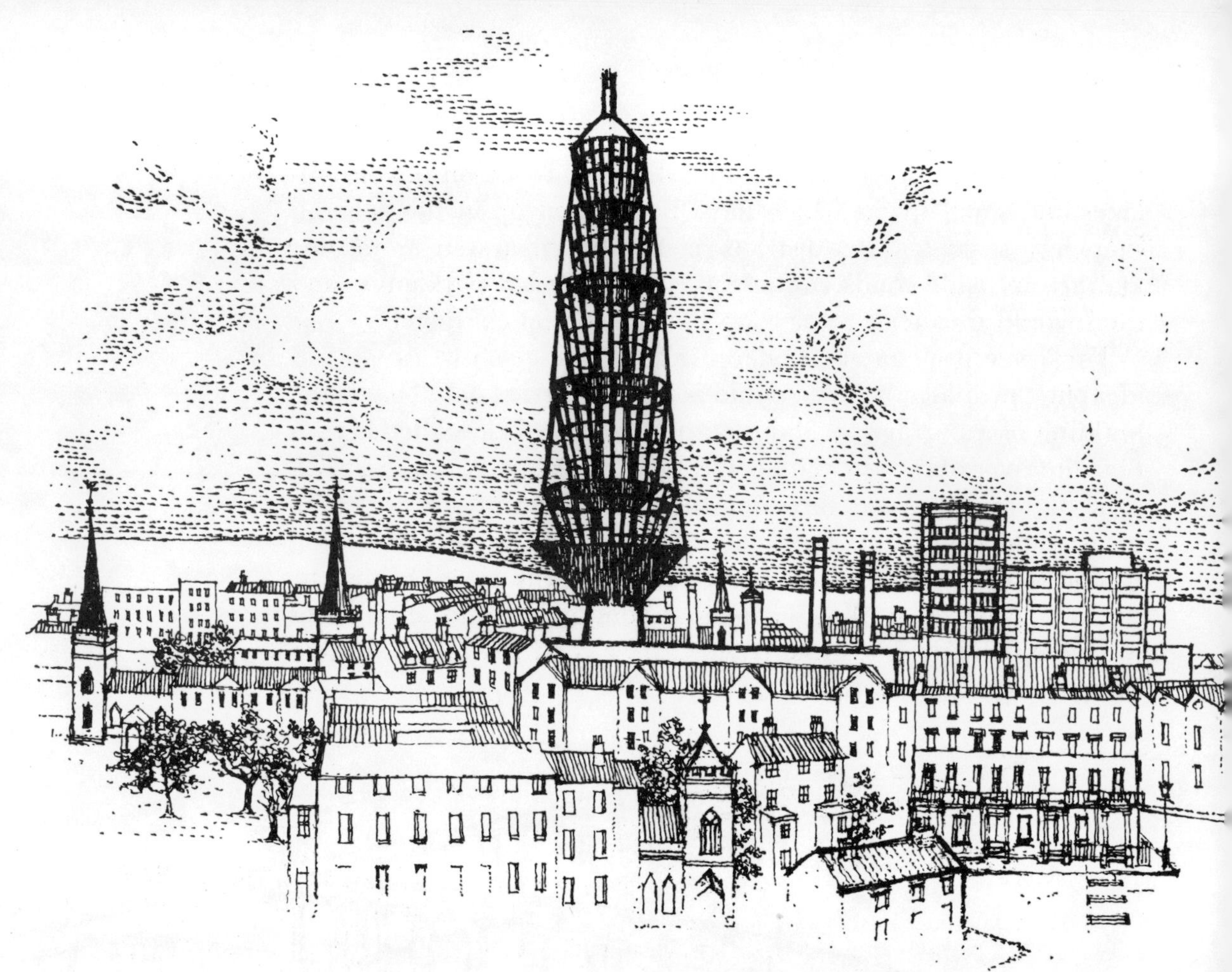

An exhibition tower of the future, 1,000 feet high, with a restaurant at the top. From a design by Ove Arup and G. A. Jellicoe for the Glass Age Development Committee.

The dam would be useful in several ways. It would mean that ships and boats could use the river above the dam at any time, without bothering about the rise and fall of the water caused by the tides; they could approach the quays in deep water at any time, and would never have to lie, straining their hulls, upon the mud when the tide was low. The dirty bed of the river would not be revealed twice a day as it is now, and the water would always be high and deep from bank to bank. Water sports of all kinds would be possible, regattas and pageants could be held as brilliant as they once were, and the fish would return. Passenger boats and smaller pleasure craft could use the river far more than they do now, and the whole of London's river would become as lively and colourful as it was in the past. It would serve, once again, as a broad and splendid high-street. What is more, London would at last be released from the old, recurring danger of flooding.

Districts along the river could make the most of their position, with open places, like the old pleasure gardens, by the banks, with wide river steps running down to landing stages by the water's edge. Some buildings, with generous, flower-filled balconies and hanging gardens, might project right over the river. Promenades, some covered over like a ship's lower decks, might run along the riverside, where people could stroll without suffering the stink, din and danger of motor traffic.

We could learn from old London, and use the best ideas of every age. For example, we could build bridges with houses along both sides, like Old London Bridge. We could make parts of the City as intricate with passages, twists, turns and surprises, as mediaeval London was, but without the poverty, dirt and squalor. We could have calm squares of terrace houses surrounding gardens, like the seventeenth and eighteenth centuries built. We might have new ideas of our own, made possible by the new skills and materials of building—tall, elegant, revolving towers, a quarter of a mile high, and gigantic, transparent domes, thin as eggshells, covering winter play-grounds half a mile across.

With the development of new and better ideas of how to live with machines, London and its riverside would improve as if by magic. Londoners could quote again with pride the line of the poet, William Dunbar:

'London, thou art the flower of cities all.'

Index

Books for Further Reading

ORMSBY, H. *London on the Thames: A Study of the Natural Conditions that Influenced the Birth and Growth of a Great City* Sifton, Praed, London. 1924

BARTON, N. J. *The Lost Rivers of London* Phoenix House, London. 1962

MITTON, G. E. *Maps of Old London* Adam & Charles Black, London. 1908

London Museum Catalogue *London in Roman Times.* 1946

STOW, JOHN *A Survey of London* First published 1598. Routledge, London, 1893

BELLOC, HILAIRE *The River of London* Foulis, London. 1912

HOME, GORDON *Old London Bridge* The Bodley Head, London. 1931

PEVSNER, N. *London: The Cities of London and Westminster* Penguin Books, Harmondsworth. 1957

WROTH, WARWICK *The London Pleasure Gardens of the Eighteenth Century* Macmillan, London. 1896

MARÉ, ERIC DE *The Bridges of Britain* Batsford, London. 1954

MARÉ, ERIC DE *London's Riverside: Past, Present and Future* Max Reinhardt, London. 1958

HOLDEN, C. H. and HOLFORD, W. G. *The City of London: A Record of Destruction and Survival with a Report on Reconstruction by the Planning Consultants* Architectural Press, London. 1947